SONGS FOR THE CYCLE

SONGS FOR THE CYCLE

FRESH HYMN TEXTS FOR CHURCH YEARS A, B & C

MICHAEL HUDSON

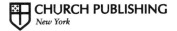

Copyright © 2004 by Michael Hudson. All rights reserved.

Portions of this book may be reproduced by a congregation for its own use. Commercial or large-scale reproduction, or reproduction for sale, of any portion of this book or of the book as a whole, without the written permission of the copyright owner is prohibited. All inquiries should be sent to the publisher at the address below.

Library of Congress Cataloging-in-Publication Data

Hudson, Michael.
    Songs for the cycle : fresh hymn texts / Michael Hudson.
      p. cm.
    Includes index.
    ISBN 0-89869-419-1 (pbk.)
    1. Episcopal Church – Hymns – Texts. 2. Episcopal Church. Lectionary (1979) 3. Hymns, English – United States – Texts. I. Title.
    BV372.H78 2004
    264'.23 – dc22

                                                                                                    2004007192

Church Publishing Incorporated
445 Fifth Avenue
New York, NY 10016
www.churchpublishing.org

5 4 3 2 1

Contents

Preface	vii
Year A	1
Year B	61
Year C	119
Additional Hymns for the Revised Common Lectionary	176
Index of Hymn Tunes	178
Thematic Index	179

PREFACE

This collection of 153 new hymn texts began on a sabbatical I took with my family to Wales, the three of us from a St. David's in North Carolina visiting St. David's Cathedral on the far western edge of Britain. The deeply refreshing pace we experienced there, the people, the culture, the farms, sheep, the breathtakingly beautiful rocky coast and, underlying everything, the profound sense of a rich spiritual past ever present in a land of stone churches and the saints whose names they bear — all this came together to make such an outrageous idea, to write a hymn a week for three years, seem possible, appealing, perhaps even inescapable.

Every creative process also has a broader context. I am an Episcopalian, and this work is certainly shaped by Anglican liturgical experience. I studied English in college, and in the years following made a living writing lyrics and jingles in Nashville, Tennessee, and so have come to appreciate not only Donne and Herbert, Keats and Yeats, Shakespeare and Shaw, but also the brevity, humor, and payoff of, say, a Burma Shave ad.

This collection, begun in Wales, continued at home in North Carolina over the subsequent three years, as week by week I wrote a text to complement the appointed gospel. Every Sunday we (St. David's, Cullowhee) sang a text set to a familiar tune. It was a wonderful, if demanding, rhythm, the weekly deadline present as both consistent encouragement and occasional terror. Every week the aim was the same, in Emily Dickinson's phrase, to "tell all the truth, but tell it slant." In other words, to catch something of the genius of the gospels in a fresh and engaging way and to do it positively, broadly, and inclusively.

As far as others using these texts, individuals can read them weekly as meditations; congregations and choirs, it is energetically hoped, will choose to sing them on various Sundays of the three-year cycle. The texts are arranged according to the Episcopal lectionary. There is also an index of hymn tunes and an index ordered by theme. Most of the texts are very obviously keyed to the lesson, though some take a more oblique approach. A few texts are used more than once. The suggested tunes for all but one can be found in the Episcopal *Hymnal 1982*. Most tunes will be familiar to those who know this hymnal. A number of the tunes are repeated — especially some of the simpler ones. You are certainly encouraged to try other tunes as well.

Permission for Copying and Congregational Use

Purchase of this volume carries with it an authorization for congregations to reproduce the texts in service leaflets, as long as the following copyright notice is included on each copy:

> From *Songs for the Cycle* © 2004 by Michael Hudson. Church Publishing Incorporated. All rights reserved. Used by permission.

Commercial reproduction, or reproduction for sale, of any portion of this book without permission of the copyright owner is expressly prohibited. Any questions about appropriate use of permission for commercial reproduction should be addressed to Church Publishing Incorporated, copyrights@cpg.org.

Acknowledgments

The opportunity to make some acknowledgment of thanks after completing a creative task reminds me of a haiku I read once, something to the effect,

> I could love you. Perhaps
> make you immortal. But not
> in three lines.

Tracing out the gifts of others, their visible and invisible incarnation into our lives, is such a worthwhile and large task — how does one begin? "I'd like to thank Dr. Simmons in Greenville, South Carolina, for taking such good care of me *in utero*." No. Well, maybe, but not exactly *here*. But one must begin — and end — *somewhere*.

My parents loved to sing, sang very well, and regularly took their three sons to Earle Street Baptist Church. English professors at Furman University opened eyes and heart to beauty, truth, and the spiritual quest inherent in poetry. The people at Belmont Church in Nashville worshiped God with passion, grace — and skilled *a cappella* voices. My friend Bob Farnsworth has shared his remarkable musical gifts with me with energy and joy for half a lifetime. The Anglican Communion astounds with the congregational music of Ralph Vaughan Williams, the poetry of George Herbert, the timeless grace of chant, and with the knowledge that to the seemingly immutable Protestant law of *one text one tune* numerous exceptions yet exist!

The commentaries of Raymond Brown, John Keenan, and Bill Loader, and several books by Marcus Borg, have been consistently helpful. I'm also grateful to have experienced a certain wonder in the lyrics of Richard Rodgers, Stephen Sondheim, Bob Dylan, Paul Simon, James Taylor, and Bruce Cockburn, and in the contemporary poetry of Seamus Heaney, Denise Levertov, R. S. Thomas, and Mary Oliver, to name but a few. The example and early encouragement of Carl Daw, Brian Wren, and Thomas Troeger were a big help. Very specifically, William Percy's text, "They cast their nets in Galilee," lit a fire in me to try to write other hymns that might engage mind and heart so deftly.

St. David's Episcopal Church in Cullowhee, North Carolina, is a community of hospitality, wisdom, good people, and good singing for which any mindful rector thanks God daily. Our hosts in Wales, Wil and Rosemary Rees, were a joy. Marilyn Haskel and Frank Tedeschi at Church Publishing have lent friendly and steady encouragement throughout the process. The proofreading of Barbara O'Neil and Jessica Philyaw was most welcome, as was the pastoral reading of good friend and priest Susan Sherard. My daughter, Ruth Hardie Hudson, read many of these texts aloud to me on the way to school, and the sound of her voice brought both delight and insight. My wife, Barbara Hardie, herself a skilled writer and teacher of writing, reviewed most of these lyrics during the three-year cycle and patiently offered both encouragement and razor-sharp criticism. To have such creative community and family support is a remarkable blessing.

Of course, I also want to thank God, who, like Dr. Simmons, observed me in my mother's womb and, quite apart from Dr. Simmons, knit into my bones a love of words and the linking of words in any attempt to manifest some outward and visible sign of inward and spiritual grace. For these and for the many other gifts and influences that remain unnamed, I am truly thankful.

— Michael Hudson
St. David's Day 2004

YEAR A

A General Meditation for Advent

Suitable for Years A, B, and C
77 77 77
Suggested tune: Ratisbon

1. At the turning of the year
   we return to contemplate
   seasons, cycles, signs, and times,
   sacred ground to cultivate.
   Insight often grows more clear
   at the turning of the year.

2. At the turning of the year
   waxing nights annunciate
   warmer days that promise spring,
   even as the sun migrates.
   Hope sleeps in the husk of fear
   at the turning of the year.

3. At the turning of the year
   we look back and speculate
   on the ebb and flow of life,
   asking what it indicates.
   Wisdom speaks, and some will hear
   at the turning of the year.

4. At the turning of the year
   we look forward as we wait
   for the grace of God in time,
   never early, never late,
   always distant, always here
   at the turning of the year.

From *Songs for the Cycle* © 2004 by Michael Hudson.
Church Publishing Incorporated. All rights reserved. Used by permission.

Meditation for Matthew 24.37–44

1 Advent, Year A
The days of Noah and the Son of Man
10 10 10 10
Suggested tune: *Sursum Corda*

1. The Son of Man has come and comes again,
   unfailing advent of unending grace;
   we tell the stories so that we may see
   the character of Incarnation's face.

2. As Noah watched the skies and built an ark
   to rise and ride above a flooded plain,
   we also hope for eyes to see the storm
   but never hearts that pray for flooding rain.

3. A proverb paints two people side by side:
   one will be taken and the other left;
   neither will live in unencumbered joy:
   each by the other's absence is bereft.

4. The Son of Man has come and comes again
   to seek the deluged and the left-behind;
   we watch and wait and hope to recognize
   the face of Jesus in the present time.

From *Songs for the Cycle* © 2004 by Michael Hudson.
Church Publishing Incorporated. All rights reserved. Used by permission.

Meditation for Matthew 3.1–12

2 Advent, Year A
A voice calling in the wilderness
Common Meter
Suggested tune: *St. Flavian* (original rhythm)
or *St. Anne*

1 Our road runs through a wilderness,
   a realm of wanderings;
   beneath a silent, desert sun
   the spirit finds its springs.

2 Each soul must make the exodus
   through sacred, arid space
   and stack the hallelujah stones
   that mark the promised place.

3 We do not pass this way alone
   but in profound array;
   the wise, the peaceable, the just
   are never far away.

4 In time we cherish desert roads,
   the slow, demanding pace;
   we are a people turned to God
   by thirst as well as grace.

From *Songs for the Cycle* © 2004 by Michael Hudson.
Church Publishing Incorporated. All rights reserved. Used by permission.

Meditation for Matthew 11.2–11

3 Advent, Year A
John asks, "Are you the one?"
CM
Suggested tune: *St. Stephen* or *St. Anne*

1. We wait for Christ, our Advent Light,
   a brightness like the sun;
   we find a rabbi with a lamp
   and ask, "Is this the One?"

2. We wait for Christ, the Lord of hosts,
   a thousand battles won;
   we find a stubborn man of peace
   and ask, "Is this the One?"

3. We wait for Christ, our Advocate,
   for justice swiftly done;
   we find a friend of the oppressed
   and ask, "Is this the One?"

4. We wait for Christ, the King of kings,
   a nation's favored son;
   we find instead a servant-sage
   and ask, "Is this the One?"

5. And so he comes, again he comes,
   and faith is yet begun
   as open hearts are drawn to Christ,
   the Unexpected One.

From *Songs for the Cycle* © 2004 by Michael Hudson.
Church Publishing Incorporated. All rights reserved. Used by permission.

Meditation for Matthew 1.18–25

4 Advent, Year A
Prophecy of Emmanuel
Common Meter
Suggested tune: *Tallis' Ordinal*

1. We hear the name Emmanuel
   down centuries of praise;
   it points us to the miracle
   the holy name conveys.

2. Isaiah prophesied the sign:
   a woman giving birth.
   He saw the day the Life of God
   would burst upon the earth.

3. When Joseph learned of Mary's child
   at first his heart was torn,
   but then he dreamed that it was God
   who waited to be born.

4. And now we sing Emmanuel
   as all the saints before
   to celebrate the miracle,
   God-with-us evermore!

From *Songs for the Cycle* © 2004 by Michael Hudson.
Church Publishing Incorporated. All rights reserved. Used by permission.

Meditation for the Sunday after Christmas

Year A
Christ is born
Common Meter Double
Suggested tune: *Kingsfold* or *Halifax*

1. Beneath a dark, familiar sky
   the silent air was stirred;
   a sudden rush like many wings
   announced a startling word:
   a word more distant than the stars
   above the stony ground
   and closer than the beating hearts
   that marked the sudden sound.

2. The shepherds rose to face the sky,
   then turned and fell face down;
   this night it seemed that Life itself
   was pressing toward the ground
   to take, to hold, to celebrate
   the substance of the earth
   and gather all creation in
   a reconciling birth.

3. The stars aligned to point a path,
   the shepherds rose and ran,
   swept up in an epiphany
   they longed to understand.
   This longing also gathers us
   to rise and go with them,
   and find our way among the ways
   that meet in Bethlehem.

From *Songs for the Cycle* © 2004 by Michael Hudson.
Church Publishing Incorporated. All rights reserved. Used by permission.

Meditation for Matthew 2.1–12

2 Christmas, Year A, and the Epiphany
Journey of the Magi
Long Meter
Suggested tune: *The Eighth Tune* or *Winchester New*
(See also text for 2 Christmas, Year B)

1. God gave a star to guide the wise,
   whose hearts were open to its light;
   to follow they gave up the day
   and went as pilgrims through the night.

2. God gave the wise to praise a child,
   who lay, a secret hope, in hay;
   the wise ones worshiped openly
   then journeyed home another way.

3. God gave the child to love a world
   that noticed neither child nor light;
   but love grew up, a brighter star,
   to guide a pilgrim through the night.

From *Songs for the Cycle* © 2004 by Michael Hudson.
Church Publishing Incorporated. All rights reserved. Used by permission.

Meditation for Matthew 3.13–17

1 Epiphany, Year A
The Baptism of Jesus
77 77 77
Suggested tune: *Dix*
(See also texts for 1 Epiphany Years B and C)

1. Jesus walked without a word
   toward the Jordan's promised grace.
   By the water John looked up,
   awed to see the promised face.
   "Why," he said, "Lord, come to me?"
   Jesus answered, "Let it be!"

2. Let the broken ones be healed.
   Let the lost be found and fed.
   Let the grace of God roll on.
   Let the river rise and spread.
   Step into the stream with me,
   Let God's gracious purpose be!

3. Let it be: the Spirit falls,
   consecrating common ground.
   Let it be: the Word of God
   whispers, thunders, soothes, resounds.
   Come, be baptized, friends, with me
   in the joy of letting be!

From *Songs for the Cycle* © 2004 by Michael Hudson.
Church Publishing Incorporated. All rights reserved. Used by permission.

Meditation for John 1.29–41

2 Epiphany, Year A
John's disciples go with Jesus
Irregular Meter
Suggested tune: *The Water Is Wide**

1. The grace of God is like a road
   that draws the heart from its first home —
   We long to go, but we hate to leave,
   and the Spirit calls, "Come follow me."

2. The voice of God is like the wind,
   it comes and goes and comes again —
   We read the signs in the bending trees,
   and the Spirit calls, "Come follow me."

3. The strength of God is like a stone;
   it firms the will of soul and bone —
   Still soul and bone grow worn and weak,
   and the Spirit calls, "Come follow me."

4. The hope of God is like the sun;
   it shines until the day is done —
   And in the night stars rise in the East,
   and the Spirit calls, "Come follow me."

5. The love of God is like a stream;
   it fills and feeds our deepest dreams —
   It finds a thirst and leaves a spring,
   and the Spirit calls, "Come follow me."

6. The peace of God is like a friend
   who sees us through the journey's end —
   The road is long and the talk is sweet,
   and the Spirit calls, "Come follow me."

*Various arrangements for "The Water Is Wide" are readily available in stores or on the Internet.

From *Songs for the Cycle* © 2004 by Michael Hudson.
Church Publishing Incorporated. All rights reserved. Used by permission.

Meditation for Matthew 4.12–23

3 Epiphany, Year A
Jesus takes up John's message
76 76
Suggested tune: *Ave caeli janua*

1   A silence which was broken
    by John's astounding word
    returned again to muffle
    all passion where it stirred.

2   A people lately singing
    now strained their hearts to hear
    the sweet, receding music,
    "the realm of God is near."

3   But hope, hushed and imprisoned,
    will not be silent long —
    another seized the promise
    and sang it, sure and strong.

4   And many joined the singing,
    and many came to hear,
    and many soon discovered
    the realm of God is near.

From *Songs for the Cycle* © 2004 by Michael Hudson.
Church Publishing Incorporated. All rights reserved. Used by permission.

Meditation for Matthew 5.1–12

4 Epiphany, Year A
The Sermon on the Mount
Common Meter Double
Suggested tune: *Forest Green* or *Halifax*

1. When Jesus scaled the mount of God
   all heaven marked his climb
   and cheered the words that rearranged
   Earth's settled paradigm.
   It was a day the devil raged,
   a day kings cursed their crowns,
   that day when all the down went up
   and all the up came down.

2. The poor and hungry went with Christ
   and savored all he said.
   The weeping came to laugh and see
   a world stood on its head.
   The hated climbed the mountain, too,
   to stand on friendly ground,
   that day when all the down went up
   and all the up came down.

3. The mountain calls its pilgrims still
   to its epiphanies,
   to gather on the heights and pray
   to see what Jesus sees:
   a world that longs to turn to God
   and, longing, comes around
   to praise the day the down go up
   and all the up come down.

From *Songs for the Cycle* © 2004 by Michael Hudson.
Church Publishing Incorporated. All rights reserved. Used by permission.

Meditation for Matthew 5.13–20

5 Epiphany, Year A
You are the light of the world
87 87
Suggested tune: *Omni die* or *Stuttgart*

1. In a simple desert dwelling
   where few windows break the gloom,
   one small lamp upon a table
   drives the darkness from a room.

2. In the clear air of the desert
   for a traveler in the night
   every lamp lit in the city
   is a soul-sustaining sight.

3. In the darkness we encounter
   where a people long for light,
   God is present to ignite us
   and illuminate the night.

From *Songs for the Cycle* © 2004 by Michael Hudson.
Church Publishing Incorporated. All rights reserved. Used by permission.

Meditation for Matthew 17.1–9

Last Epiphany, Year A
The Mount of Transfiguration
10 9 10 9 D (1 note=1 syllable)
Suggested tune: *Pleading Savior*

1. Sometimes we come to the soul's high places,
   groping or led by a wiser hand,
   taken beyond our familiar limits,
   witnessing more than we understand.
   Singular insights spring up unsummoned,
   torah and story find form and flesh,
   hope rises up and soars unencumbered
   here where the bound and the Boundless mesh.

2. Breached are the walls of the fixed and patterned,
   burst are the banks that divert the flood,
   in streams the tide of the gleaming Spirit
   lighting the earth with its bright lifeblood.
   Even the ground where, kneeling, we settle
   warms with the glow of radiant light:
   Never again, thinks a changed disciple,
   must we encounter the cold, stark night.

3. Ah! We would stay where the glory thunders,
   worship and pray while the spirit burns,
   if we did not in the mind's eye notice
   how resolutely the Spirit turns.
   Tracing the footsteps that led us upward
   back to the ways where warmed hearts will break,
   we find compassion and God's hand moving
   on toward the place where a worn world wakes.

From Songs for the Cycle © 2004 by Michael Hudson.
Church Publishing Incorporated. All rights reserved. Used by permission.

Meditation for Matthew 4.1–11

1 Lent, Year A
The temptation of Jesus
87 87 87
Suggested tune: *Julion* or *Lauda anima*

1. "Lead us not into temptation,"
   Jesus teaches us to pray,
   recognizing how the tempter
   works to bend us from the way
   that is open to the promise
   and the purpose of each day.

2. "Lead us not into temptation,"
   Jesus guides a heart to cry
   when the devil comes enticing,
   spinning visions in the sky.
   Wisdom knows an easy journey
   is the devil's sweetest lie.

3. "Lead us not into temptation,"
   Jesus understands the prayer.
   Still he points us toward the desert
   with its devils, well aware
   God is sending better angels
   on the wind to join us there.

From *Songs for the Cycle* © 2004 by Michael Hudson.
Church Publishing Incorporated. All rights reserved. Used by permission.

Meditation for John 3.1–17

2 Lent, Year A
"You must be born again"
Common Meter
Suggested tune: *St. Flavian*

1. A font evokes the womb of God,
a place the soul takes form
in rhythm with the pulsing heart,
kept safe and fed and warm.

2. But soon enough the water breaks
and sleeping souls, uncurled,
are pushed with unrelenting will
into a waiting world.

3. Unlike the warm, sustaining womb,
this hard, demanding earth —
it is a terrifying gift,
the miracle of birth.

4. But baptized, born of God we are;
the new imprint is deep,
and children who awake to God
will not return to sleep...

5. But seek to grow as all things grow
and trust what grace assumes —
that time will manifest the Life
received within the womb.

From *Songs for the Cycle* © 2004 by Michael Hudson.
Church Publishing Incorporated. All rights reserved. Used by permission.

Meditation for John 4:5–26 (27–38) 39–42

3 Lent, Year A
Jesus and a Samaritan woman at Jacob's Well
Common Meter
Suggested tune: *Dundee*

1 The grace of God desires to be
   where custom holds it down;
   beneath the old, determined feet
   grace rises from the ground.

2 Two people met at Jacob's Well,
   Samaritan and Jew,
   and centuries of prejudice
   prescribed what each would do.

3 Instead the one invited talk,
   the other spoke her mind,
   and something fresh welled up to quench
   thirst of the deepest kind.

4 The grace of God desires to be
   where custom holds it down;
   beneath the old, determined feet
   grace rises from the ground.

From *Songs for the Cycle* © 2004 by Michael Hudson.
Church Publishing Incorporated. All rights reserved. Used by permission.

Meditation for John 9

4 Lent, Year A
Jesus heals a man born blind
87 87 Double
Suggested tune: *Nettleton*

1. Darkness lay upon the waters,
   and the starless heavens swirled
   as the formless earth awaited
   the creating of a world.
   Over all the Spirit brooded
   like a patient mother bird
   for the leaping of the morning
   at the speaking of a Word.

2. In another age of darkness
   children stumbled, blind from birth,
   as the Word of God, incarnate,
   moved again upon the earth
   with the re-creating promise
   that the sightless would be healed
   and perceive the new creation
   that the light of God revealed.

3. Every soul will sit with darkness,
   every eye will long for light,
   every heart will lose direction
   in the swirling, starless night.
   Still the One who speaks the morning
   moves beside us on the way;
   knowing this we know that darkness
   always holds the hope of day.

From *Songs for the Cycle* © 2004 by Michael Hudson.
Church Publishing Incorporated. All rights reserved. Used by permission.

Meditation for John 11.(1–16) 17–44

5 Lent, Year A
The raising of Lazarus
77 77 77
Suggested tune: Ratisbon

1. When the first disciples saw
   Jesus, Lamb of God, pass by
   they were drawn to know the light
   that he came to amplify.
   Coaxing their epiphany,
   Jesus bid them, "Come and see."

2. With their brother four days dead
   two worn sisters saw the Lord.
   He was late and they were grieved
   that their prayers appeared ignored.
   Near a tomb in Bethany,
   they bid Jesus, "Come and see."

3. Sometimes it is Christ who calls,
   Come and see the rising light.
   Sometimes it is we who cry,
   Come and see our long, dark night.
   In both bright and shadowed place
   we meet God's life-changing grace.

From *Songs for the Cycle* © 2004 by Michael Hudson.
Church Publishing Incorporated. All rights reserved. Used by permission.

Meditation for Matthew 26–27

Palm Sunday, Year A
Jesus enters Jerusalem
LM
Suggested tune: *Winchester New*
(See also text for 5 Lent, Year B)

1. We raise our branches high today
   to sign Hosanna and to warn:
   The hands that wield a waving branch
   may also weave a crown of thorns.

2. We sing exultant songs today,
   yet singing we remember this:
   The lips that bring the sweetest praise
   may also bear the sharpest kiss.

3. We greet a golden dawn today
   and marvel as the darkness grows
   that even stalwart confidence
   may fail before the rooster crows.

4. And so our hearts are shaped today
   by palms, a kiss, a friend's denial,
   to hold the very simple prayer—
   God, save us from the time of trial.

From *Songs for the Cycle* © 2004 by Michael Hudson.
Church Publishing Incorporated. All rights reserved. Used by permission.

Meditation for Matthew's Resurrection Narrative

Easter Day, Year A, especially appropriate for a Vigil service
The burial and resurrection of Jesus
11 11 11 11
Suggested tune: *Adoro devote*

1. In the second darkness of the dying day
   Joseph comes for Jesus, bearing him away,
   not with bright hosannas toward a royal throne
   but with dark emotion toward a hollowed stone.

2. Gathered on the Sabbath, guards stand by a tomb
   fearing shrewd disciples coming to exhume
   Christ, a bold deception: See the empty cave!
   Sword and stone and cunning seal a silent grave.

3. Then as bright as lightning power shakes the earth,
   intervening angel as at Jesus' birth,
   present for a purpose, here to show a door
   closed one bitter moment, open evermore.

From *Songs for the Cycle* © 2004 by Michael Hudson.
Church Publishing Incorporated. All rights reserved. Used by permission.

Meditation for John 20.19–31

2 Easter, Years A, B, and C
Jesus appears to Thomas
10 10 10 10
Suggested tune: *Nyack*

1. I have not seen, how am I to believe?
   My eyes have never marked the risen Christ.
   Is one to trust the stories others tell,
   God raising up what has been sacrificed?

2. I have not felt his hands, stone cold, grow warm,
   nor heard the heart once silenced beat again;
   yet here I am, surrounded by a faith
   that apprehends his presence now as then.

3. We hope for signs, but in the end will trust
   that risen Life, arising, surely weaves
   of faith and doubt alike a living truth
   that blesses all who question to believe.

From *Songs for the Cycle* © 2004 by Michael Hudson.
Church Publishing Incorporated. All rights reserved. Used by permission.

MEDITATION FOR LUKE 24.13–35

3 Easter, Year A
The road to Emmaus
Long Meter
Suggested tune: *The Eighth Tune*
(See also text for 3 Easter, Year B)

1. Two travelers left Jerusalem,
   their deepest hope unrealized.
   They thought life had been snatched away,
   but Life was there, unrecognized.

2. The two had clues that God was near,
   they spoke their anguish and were heard.
   And when the stranger turned to speak,
   it was a living, burning Word.

3. And there were signs of hope renewed
   by nightfall that first Easter day,
   the two encountered such delight
   they importuned Delight to stay.

4. The stranger stayed to share a meal—
   this one they'd thought was three days dead.
   And here at last they recognized
   Christ in the breaking of the bread.

From *Songs for the Cycle* © 2004 by Michael Hudson.
Church Publishing Incorporated. All rights reserved. Used by permission.

Meditation for John 10.1–10

4 Easter, Year A
"My sheep hear my voice"
Long Meter
Suggested tune: The Eighth Tune
(See also text for 4 Easter, Year C)

1. Among the day's competing sounds
   that roar or murmur, numb, confound,
   we wonder, here with so much noise,
   how people ever hear God's voice.

2. And then we pray and think we might
   detect a spark of spoken light.
   Or savoring a certain word,
   we think, Yes, this is God we've heard.

3. Or in our common liturgy
   we find a sacred energy
   that shapes the opportunity
   to hear God in community.

4. Or in the people that we meet,
   the friend or stranger that we greet,
   we sense some *thing* we need to do
   and hear in this God speaking, too.

5. And after listening in such ways,
   and at the end of noisy days,
   we recollect and then rejoice.
   Again, by grace, we've heard God's voice.

From *Songs for the Cycle* © 2004 by Michael Hudson.
Church Publishing Incorporated. All rights reserved. Used by permission.

Meditation for John 14.1–14

5 Easter, Year A
"In my Father's House are many rooms"
87 87
Suggested tune: *Restoration* or *Stuttgart*

1. Many rooms await a seeker
   summoned by God's gracious call—
   in the heart of the Creator
   there is room enough for all.

2. All who undertake the journey,
   yearning, growing, straining, stressed,
   find in God a will for living
   and in God a blessed rest.

3. Rest within the day's adventure,
   shelter in both joy and strife,
   peace past common understanding
   in this Way, this Truth, this Life.

4. Life awaits us and attends us,
   Life, beside, within, above,
   dwells with us in time and ever
   binds us in a boundless love.

From *Songs for the Cycle* © 2004 by Michael Hudson.
Church Publishing Incorporated. All rights reserved. Used by permission.

Meditation for John 15.1–8

6 Easter, Year A
"I am the vine, you are the branches"
Common Meter Double
Suggested tune: *Kingsfold*

1 The keeper of a vineyard dreamed
   of vines alive with fruit
   and tended vine and dream alike
   down years of sharp dispute,
   as others came to claim the land,
   to drink its fruit as spoil,
   without a grower's love of growth
   or farmer's love of soil.

2 The keeper had a child, firstborn,
   who came to work the land.
   The malcontents desired his life
   but did not understand—
   this life, once it was given up,
   this blood, once spilled like wine,
   would soak deep down into the ground
   and rise up in the vine.

3 And then the plant, fresh charged, would be
   itself a vein of grace,
   a way the keeper might extend
   a hopeful, green embrace,
   connecting child and foe and friend,
   co-mingled and entwined,
   to be and bear the fruit of God
   in one life-giving vine.

From *Songs for the Cycle* © 2004 by Michael Hudson.
Church Publishing Incorporated. All rights reserved. Used by permission.

Meditation for John 17.1–17

7 Easter, Year A
"Eternal Life is this..."
Common Meter
Suggested tune: *Georgetown* or *St. Anne*

1. Eternal life is knowing God,
   and knowing God is near,
   the place we are, the path we take,
   both womb and next frontier.

2. Eternal life is doing work
   that thrills and strains the soul,
   that takes our joy, the world's deep needs
   and weaves a common goal.

3. Eternal life is loving those
   the Spirit brings our way,
   and holding dear the wealth God hides
   in every pinch of clay.

4. Eternal Life is knowing Christ,
   God with us, flesh and bone,
   and knowing God delights with us
   to make such knowledge known.

The thought in stanza two is borrowed directly from Frederick Buechner's definition of vocation.

From *Songs for the Cycle* © 2004 by Michael Hudson.
Church Publishing Incorporated. All rights reserved. Used by permission.

Meditation for John 20.19–23

Pentecost, Year A
"Receive the Holy Spirit"
11 11 11 11
Suggested tune: *St. Denio* or *Foundation*

1. Fresh fire falls from heaven, a sign from above
   that now is the moment to burn with God's love
   and carry the brightness out into the world,
   like stars through the vast, spreading universe hurled.

2. Now Wisdom is calling and gathers her friends
   to share in the movement of grace God intends.
   We come in all colors, from faraway lands,
   yet each hears a language the soul understands.

3. Praise God for this moment! and leap at the chance
   to join in the Spirit's great, spiraling dance —
   One spark lights another until all acquire
   this bright, blessed, heart-waking Pentecost fire.

From *Songs for the Cycle* © 2004 by Michael Hudson.
Church Publishing Incorporated. All rights reserved. Used by permission.

A Meditation Suitable for Trinity Sunday

87 87
Suggested tune: *Omni die*
(See also the text for Last Epiphany, Year A)

1. Every pilgrim has a mountain
   that is hers alone to climb,
   rising from the deepest places,
   standing through the rush of time.

2. Every mountain has a summit
   calling out to him who seeks,
   though the way is often winding
   and the summoning oblique.

3. Every summit has a threshold
   with a path from either side,
   where the hopeful meet the Hoped-for
   and the guided know their Guide.

4. Guide us now and guide us always,
   God of pilgrimage and peak,
   Source of all that draws and drives us,
   Sum of everything we seek.

From *Songs for the Cycle* © 2004 by Michael Hudson.
Church Publishing Incorporated. All rights reserved. Used by permission.

Meditation for Matthew 6.24–34

Proper 3, Year A
Do not worry about tomorrow
CM
Suggested tune: *Dundee*

1. A prayer can ride a breath, exhaled,
   like ashes ride a breeze
   and take away by scrap and whit
   a frazzled heart's unease.

2. There comes a time to clear a soul's
   accumulating mess,
   to trade a trove of bother for
   the gift of emptiness.

3. When Peter was a fisherman
   he found, for all his skill,
   it's often not the brimming boat
   Christ purposes to fill.

4. God, give us breath that carries off
   the refuse of the day
   and finds our lightened, anchored souls
   uncluttered as we pray.

From *Songs for the Cycle* © 2004 by Michael Hudson.
Church Publishing Incorporated. All rights reserved. Used by permission.

Meditation for Matthew 7.21–27 (Option 1)

Proper 4, Year A
A wise builder
Irr.
Suggested tune: *Shalom chevarim*
(Especially for children)

1 We'll build a house,
we'll build a house,
upon a rock.
Upon a rock
we'll build a house,
upon a rock.

2 The storms may come,
and rain may fall,
the wind may blow;
but our good house,
yes, our good house
will stand, will stand.

3 Our house will stand,
our house will stand
on God's strong love.
On God's strong love
our house will stand,
on God's strong love

The first verse may be repeated.

From *Songs for the Cycle* © 2004 by Michael Hudson.
Church Publishing Incorporated. All rights reserved. Used by permission.

Meditation for Matthew 7.21–27 (Option 2)

Proper 4, Year A
The wise builder
Wisdom's role in our choices is amplified
88
Suggested tune: *Come, Holy Ghost* (first section)

1 Come, Wisdom: teacher, guide, midwife,
and bring with you the friends of life.

2 Bring Silence: fertile garden earth,
who sings the dreams of God to birth.

3 Bring Stillness: in whose vastness grow
the seeds of all a mind can know.

4 Bring Patience: grace of God who waits,
and moves with God when God creates.

5 Bring Kindness: who exults to share
the gifts, the grace, the life we bear.

6 Bring Justice: supple, active one,
who with us wills God's kindness done.

7 Come, Wisdom: teacher, guide midwife,
and bring with you the friends of life.

From *Songs for the Cycle* © 2004 by Michael Hudson.
Church Publishing Incorporated. All rights reserved. Used by permission.

Meditation for Matthew 9.9–13

Proper 5, Year A
"Why does your teacher
eat with tax collectors and sinners?"
Long Meter
Suggested tune: *Winchester New*

1. Why is it that the friends of God
   seem such a mixed and motley lot?
   What hand stirs such variety
   into a solitary pot?

2. How is it that the love we meet
   astonishes by being wide?
   What sanctuary can there be
   if only some may come inside?

3. Why does the One we follow first
   come first to disenfranchised folk?
   What striking hospitality
   attends the Name that we invoke!

From *Songs for the Cycle* © 2004 by Michael Hudson.
Church Publishing Incorporated. All rights reserved. Used by permission.

Meditation for Matthew 9.35–10.8

Proper 6, Year A
"Pray to the Lord of the harvest to send laborers"
Long Meter
Suggested tune: *Dickinson College*

1. Our better prayers begin as love,
   with hearts awake to human need;
   compassion, when it has its way,
   will find a way to intercede.

2. As Jesus walked from town to town,
   he saw more hurt than he could heal;
   so love recast itself as prayer
   and watched for God to be revealed.

3. Soon others joined with him to pray:
   "The need is great, O God, send aid!"
   And love sprang up again as these
   themselves became the prayers they prayed.

From *Songs for the Cycle* © 2004 by Michael Hudson.
Church Publishing Incorporated. All rights reserved. Used by permission.

Meditation for Matthew 10.16–33

Proper 7, Year A
"What I say in the dark, tell in the light"
Common Meter
Suggested tune: *St. Anne*

1. We need not shrink in time of trial
   or curse an enemy;
   in crisis Jesus gathered strength,
   and so, by grace, can we.

2. The Word of God is always near
   to strengthen and to bless;
   it is attention that improves
   when we are in distress.

3. There is a deep, abiding truth
   that only comes to light
   when people, for the love of God,
   contend for what is right.

4. So when injustice muffles truth
   we may, by faith, rejoice —
   The Word which was and always is
   will help us find our voice.

From *Songs for the Cycle* © 2004 by Michael Hudson.
Church Publishing Incorporated. All rights reserved. Used by permission.

Meditation for Matthew 10.34–42

Proper 8, Year A
"Who receives you receives me"
Meter: Long Meter
Suggested tune: *Puer nobis*

1. There is a circle like a crown
   that spirals up and spirals down,
   a golden cord that joins us all,
   the strong and weak, the great and small.

2. Filled up with God, the Savior fills
   his friends with God, and God instills
   in them a will to take and share
   the bright and blessed Gift they bear.

3. And those receiving gifts from them
   receive, as well, the gift of him
   who sends, like angels from above,
   a rushing wind of bracing love.

4. And all who share the gifts they get
   begin repayment of the debt,
   "For all you give the least of these,
   you give," the Savior says, "to me!"

5. There is a circle like a crown
   that spirals up and spirals down,
   a golden cord that joins us all,
   the strong and weak, the great and small.

From *Songs for the Cycle* © 2004 by Michael Hudson.
Church Publishing Incorporated. All rights reserved. Used by permission.

Meditation for Matthew 11.25–30

Proper 9, Year A
"You have hidden these things from the wise
and revealed them to little children"
10 10 10 10
Suggested tune: *Sursum Corda*

1. There is a wisdom that betrays the soul,
 a thousands truths, a few decisive lies
 dressed in the finery of righteousness,
 the settled tenets pupils memorize.

2. There is a wisdom that awakes the soul,
 a rising path that shimmers with surprise.
 God gives us eyes as wide as children's are
 so we can take the way that makes us wise.

From *Songs for the Cycle* © 2004 by Michael Hudson.
Church Publishing Incorporated. All rights reserved. Used by permission.

Meditation for Matthew 13.1–9; 18–23

Proper 10, Year A
The parable of the sower
Common Meter
Suggested tune: Irish

1. God is extravagant with seed
   and scatters it about,
   so as it settles far and near
   a few will always sprout.

2. We are extravagant with ground
   and casual with seeds;
   too frequently a willing earth
   grows thick and green with weeds.

3. Yet every day a billion times
   a wonder will unfold
   as God's good seed finds our good soil,
   and Life, again, takes hold.

From *Songs for the Cycle* © 2004 by Michael Hudson.
Church Publishing Incorporated. All rights reserved. Used by permission.

Meditation for Matthew 13.24–30, 36–43

Proper 11, Year A
The parable of the wheat and the weeds
87 87
Suggested tune: *St. Columba*

1. The roots of all things interweave
   and grow so close together
   that when we pull the crowding weed
   the wheat is also severed.

2. The hummingbird that works its wings
   to hover near a flower
   will aid the wind that drives the cloud
   that forms the distant shower.

3. Along with God we co-create
   a vast, connecting story
   and shape a common destiny
   and trail a common glory.

4. The world is one community,
   bound root and soul forever;
   and if we are to grow at all,
   we all must grow together.

From *Songs for the Cycle* © 2004 by Michael Hudson.
Church Publishing Incorporated. All rights reserved. Used by permission.

Meditation for Matthew 13:31–33, 44–49A

Proper 12, Year A
Parables of the Kingdom
Long Meter
Suggested tune: *The Eighth Tune*

1. A woman took a pinch of yeast
   and hid it in a mound of dough;
   she used a great amount of meal,
   enough to make a hundred loaves.

2. Her action likely caused offense
   (the righteous used unrisen bread);
   and yet she leavened all the dough
   and waited as it rose and spread.

3. It was the measure Sarah used
   when God came unexpectedly;
   it often takes extravagance
   to celebrate epiphany.

4. This woman, Jesus tells the crowd,
   reveals the realm of God with yeast!
   By adding in what most leave out
   she sets a Messianic feast.

From *Songs for the Cycle* © 2004 by Michael Hudson.
Church Publishing Incorporated. All rights reserved. Used by permission.

Meditation for Matthew 14.13–21

Proper 13, Year A
Jesus' compassion for the five thousand
Common Meter
Suggested tune: *St. Anne*

1. When circumstances drain the soul
   to leave us dry as sand,
   compassion understands the way
   to fill us up again.

2. When Jesus learned that John was dead
   he sought a lonely place;
   instead he found a teeming crowd
   who ran to him for grace.

3. The people brought ten thousand needs
   and waited to be fed,
   and Jesus, for the love of God,
   was willing to be bread.

4. God, show us in our emptiness
   that there is grace to spare
   each time we take the bread we have,
   look up, give thanks, and share.

From *Songs for the Cycle* © 2004 by Michael Hudson.
Church Publishing Incorporated. All rights reserved. Used by permission.

Meditation for Matthew 14.22–33

Proper 14, Year A
Jesus comes to his friends across the water
10 10 10 10
Suggested tune: *Nyack*

1. There will be times when Christ seems far away
   and we alone upon a restless sea;
   but faith can speak through wind and wave to say,
   The truth is deeper than what seems to be.

2. There will be times when Christ is walking near
   and yet some play of light may hide Light's face;
   bright eyes can fail and glory yet appear
   as other senses wake to welcome grace.

3. There will be times when Christ inspires great deeds,
   and we will leave our boats to brave the sea
   and surely sink, though sinking, still succeed
   each time we come when Christ says, Come to me.

From *Songs for the Cycle* © 2004 by Michael Hudson.
Church Publishing Incorporated. All rights reserved. Used by permission.

Meditation for Matthew 15.21–28

Proper 15, Year A
A Gentile woman intercedes for her daughter
10 10 10 10
Suggested tune: *Sursum Corda* or *Flentge*

1. A Gentile woman came to Christ to glean
   the leavings of the Messianic Feast,
   and Jesus marked her loud, determined prayer
   and his disciples' cry her prayer should cease.

2. She came alone, a native foreigner,
   and made no claim of kin or common creed.
   She only brought a parent's simple plea:
   her child was sick and she would intercede.

3. The gift she sought that day she got by faith
   that would not bend or break or turn or tire.
   And Jesus spoke the words she came to hear,
   "It shall be done for you as you desire."

From *Songs for the Cycle* © 2004 by Michael Hudson.
Church Publishing Incorporated. All rights reserved. Used by permission.

Meditation for Matthew 16.13–20

Proper 16, Year A
"Who do people say the Son of Man is?"
87 87
Suggested tune: *Stuttgart* or *Omni die*

1. What do people say of Jesus,
   now as centuries have passed —
   In the pulsing world around us,
   is the question often asked?

2. What do others' answers tell us
   of the world and of the Church —
   is the Christ of our confession
   one for whom the world would search?

3. Has the Seed the Spirit scatters
   taken root in us and grown —
   Who is Jesus? May we know him
   well enough to make him known.

From *Songs for the Cycle* © 2004 by Michael Hudson.
Church Publishing Incorporated. All rights reserved. Used by permission.

Meditation for Matthew 16.21–27

Proper 17, Year A
Take up your cross and follow me
10 10 10 10
Suggested tune: *Sursum Corda*

1. The way to Life takes unexpected turns,
   contrary to what one anticipates.
   Who plots a path through hell's uneasy streets
   to reach the peace of heaven's sturdy gates?

2. We meet the warm, transforming love of God,
   embrace and praise it, yet misunderstand
   that love, to reach and warm a wider world,
   flows often crosswise to the ways we've planned.

3. Our peace in pieces lies before our eyes:
   one piece runs with and one against the grain.
   These meet and point to heaven when we bind
   God's great love in us to the world's great pain.

From *Songs for the Cycle* © 2004 by Michael Hudson.
Church Publishing Incorporated. All rights reserved. Used by permission.

Meditation for Matthew 18.15–20

Proper 18, Year A
"If someone sins against you..."
Common Meter
Suggested tune: *St. Anne*

1. The love of God invites respect
   for all that love surveys,
   for everything that lives and is
   lives under love's wide gaze.

2. We'll never meet another soul
   who is not counted dear —
   there's not another way to count
   among God's children here.

3. Of all the hurts we give and get
   there's none so great it stands
   beyond God's active, supple love
   and reconciling hand.

4. God's tender mercies tend us well,
   and we illuminate
   the nature of the love of God
   as we reciprocate.

From *Songs for the Cycle* © 2004 by Michael Hudson.
Church Publishing Incorporated. All rights reserved. Used by permission.

Meditation for Matthew 18.21–35

Proper 19, Year A
"How many times shall I forgive"
10 10 10 10
Suggested tune: *Flentge*

1. Forgiveness is a given with the Lord,
   no matter how much injury is stored;
   it doesn't matter where the process starts,
   God's mercy aims to settle in our hearts.

2. We see in Jesus that a soul on fire
   can strive against injustice, yet aspire
   to burn with mercy for the very ones
   who strive to see that justice is not done.

3. We know that many often mock the meek,
   convinced too much compassion makes us weak;
   yet we, though counted meek or weak or odd,
   know that in loving mercy we find God.

From *Songs for the Cycle* © 2004 by Michael Hudson.
Church Publishing Incorporated. All rights reserved. Used by permission.

Meditation for Matthew 20.1–16

Proper 20, Year A
The parable of the laborers in the vineyard
Long Meter
Suggested tune: *The Eighth Tune*

1. A bright, unsympathetic sun
   marked off the hours one by one
   as workers hurried to a field
   to gather what the ground would yield.

2. Throughout the morning others came,
   throughout the day it was the same:
   the farmer, with a crop to get,
   hired every sturdy back he met.

3. But when the laborers were paid
   some were distressed with what was made;
   it did not matter when they'd come,
   they each received an equal sum!

4. We understand the day's dismay,
   the puzzle over equal pay;
   it's scandalous in any age
   to have compassion set the wage.

From *Songs for the Cycle* © 2004 by Michael Hudson.
Church Publishing Incorporated. All rights reserved. Used by permission.

Meditation for Matthew 21.28–32

Proper 21, Year A
The parable of the two sons and the vineyard
Long Meter
Suggested tune: *Winchester New*
or *Dickinson College*

1. It's easy to agree with God
   concerning what is right and good,
   and harder to unite with God
   to do the things we thought we would.

2. We've known the once-compelling word,
   the worthy goal, the soul's assent,
   but grow immune to what we've heard
   and distant from our heart's intent.

3. This is a journey children make,
   conditioned to a parent's voice:
   some vows we keep and some we break
   and scarcely know we've made the choice.

4. Most gracious God, help us to be
   a people gathered year by year
   who tell the Story faithfully
   and still respond to what we hear.

From *Songs for the Cycle* © 2004 by Michael Hudson.
Church Publishing Incorporated. All rights reserved. Used by permission.

MEDITATION FOR MATTHEW 21.33–43

Proper 22, Year A
The parable of the vineyard
Common Meter Double
Suggested tune: *Kingsfold*
(The Irish tune *Star of the County Down*
may also be used)

1   Because we do not see the One
    who animates all things,
    we sometimes think we own a world
    we're only fostering
    and miss the God-revealing chance
    to tend and then to share
    the time, the skill, the life, the gifts
    we find within our care.

2   God puts us on a patch of ground
    and sets us tending vines
    so we can learn the alchemy
    that changes grapes to wine,
    and greed to hospitality,
    and guardedness to grace,
    that makes of walled and fence-crossed lands
    one wide, inviting space.

3   Our ground is good, the sun is bright,
    the rain renews the land,
    and we as gracious gardeners
    enflesh God's gracious hand.
    This is the Messianic dream,
    a table richly spread
    where God, unseen, is yet perceived
    and everyone is fed.

From *Songs for the Cycle* © 2004 by Michael Hudson.
Church Publishing Incorporated. All rights reserved. Used by permission.

Meditation for Matthew 22.1–14

Proper 23, Year A
The parable of the wedding banquet
Long Meter
Suggested tune: *The Eighth Tune*

1. Before the morning light has passed
   there is a table to prepare;
   its linens will be spread in faith,
   its vessels will be placed with prayer.

2. A hand puts bread upon a plate,
   another fills a jar with wine;
   today we make a sacred feast,
   these preparations are a sign.

3. A door is opened to the world
   and candles lit expectantly;
   a cordial silence bears a voice,
   Come in my friends and eat with me!

4. And here, with everything arranged,
   before the songs and feasting start,
   we see enough to recognize
   the presence of a gracious heart.

From *Songs for the Cycle* © 2004 by Michael Hudson.
Church Publishing Incorporated. All rights reserved. Used by permission.

Meditation for Matthew 22.15–22

Proper 24, Year A
"Give Caesar what is Caesar's and God what is God's"
Common Meter
Suggested tune: *St. Anne* or *St. Flavian*
(Another text for children follows)

1. The foolish set a snare for God
   with subtle, cunning thought,
   and find that when the trap is sprung
   it's they who have been caught.

2. So many of us come in time
   to parry with the Lord,
   and then, disarmed, stand face to face
   with Wisdom's laughing sword.

3. A soul is wise to laugh along,
   discomfited by grace,
   and praise the foolishness that falls
   into God's shrewd embrace.

From *Songs for the Cycle* © 2004 by Michael Hudson.
Church Publishing Incorporated. All rights reserved. Used by permission.

Meditation for Matthew 22.15–22

Proper 24, Year A
"Give Caesar what is Caesar's and God what is God's"
(A song for children)
Common Meter
Suggested tune: *Land of Rest*

1 What shall we give to God who gives
    the birds their morning song?
    Like birds we'll give our own best voice
    and let God make it strong.

2 What shall we say to God whose Word
    moves stars across the night?
    We'll say, Please, God, make us like stars
    to fill the world with light.

3 What shall we pray to God who's heard
    a million prayers before?
    A prayer that knows that God is glad
    to hear a billion more.

4 What shall we make for God who makes
    all worlds, all things, all ways?
    A promise in our deepest hearts
    to love God all our days.

From *Songs for the Cycle* © 2004 by Michael Hudson.
Church Publishing Incorporated. All rights reserved. Used by permission.

Meditation for Matthew 22.34–46

Proper 25, Year A
Love for God and neighbor
11 11 11 11
Suggested tune: *Adoro devote*
(See also Proper 26, Year B)

1. Many choices meet us, moving through the day,
   some move on toward meaning, others lead away.
   In the day's deciding, wisdom is defined,
   as we grow to love you, God, with all our mind.

2. Many yearnings draw us in a world of things,
   dancing lights invite us, distant voices sing.
   Some desires divide us, others make us whole,
   as we grow to love you, God, with all our soul.

3. Many people join us, journeys parallel,
   friend and kin and stranger, people like ourselves
   in the sacred drama, searching for a part,
   as we grow to love you, God, with all our heart.

4. God, be in our thinking, always as a guide;
   God be in our yearning, high and deep and wide;
   God be in our caring, with us intertwined,
   as we grow to love you, heart and soul and mind.

From *Songs for the Cycle* © 2004 by Michael Hudson.
Church Publishing Incorporated. All rights reserved. Used by permission.

Meditation for Matthew 23.1–12

Proper 26, Year A
"You place heavy burdens on people
and do not help bear them"
76 76
Suggested tune: *Ave caeli janua*

1. There is a hope of turning,
   wherever people roam;
   our vagrant hearts are guided
   by that which leads us home.

2. We recognize the Spirit
   that moves toward growth and grace,
   and turn to follow freely
   a God-directed pace.

3. We've bent to harsher counsel,
   and studied what we lack,
   and tried to carry teachings
   that break a seeker's back.

4. Today we praise a Wisdom
   that buoys up the soul
   and points us to the Wonder
   that draws us toward the Goal.

From *Songs for the Cycle* © 2004 by Michael Hudson.
Church Publishing Incorporated. All rights reserved. Used by permission.

Meditation for Matthew 25.1–13

Proper 27, Year A
The parable of the ten lamps
Long Meter
Suggested tune: *The Eighth Tune*

1. A long obedience is asked
   of those who choose the way of God;
   each passage through the soul's dark night
   requires a willingness to plod.

2. And sometimes in the plodding night
   as eager hearts await renewal,
   we find that in our watchfulness
   we burn our last reserve of fuel.

3. Yet it is here, through many times
   of failing lamps and waning sight,
   we come to see the Realm of God
   between its once and future light.

4. Awaited One, replenish us
   with grace and patience, faith and fire
   to forge the long obedience
   that brings us to our heart's desire.

From *Songs for the Cycle* © 2004 by Michael Hudson.
Church Publishing Incorporated. All rights reserved. Used by permission.

Meditation for Matthew 25.14–15, 19–29

Proper 28, Year A
The parable of the talents
LM
Suggested tune: *Deus tuorum militum*
or *Winchester New*

1. To think like Jesus is to risk
   the many gifts we have from God,
   not guard or bury secretly
   our treasure in congenial sod.

2. God gives us wealth of soul to dare
   ten thousand good, creative deeds;
   still there are times when saints decline
   to grow the gifts the Spirit seeds.

3. We hold a story that explodes
   with news God's mercies never fail.
   Why speak the words as if they made
   a merely cautionary tale?

4. We can live boldly with a God
   who ventures grace so dauntlessly
   and learn to take, like Jesus did,
   the risk of generosity.

From *Songs for the Cycle* © 2004 by Michael Hudson.
Church Publishing Incorporated. All rights reserved. Used by permission.

Meditation for Matthew 25.31–46

Proper 29, Year A
"As you did it to the least of these"
10 10 10 10
Suggested tune: *Flentge* or *Nyack*

1. O Jesus, we have tried to make you King
   and hoped for crowns on earth and thrones above,
   but you resist triumphalistic dreams
   and bring instead a majesty of love.

2. We wait the day when "Christ the King" descends
   and all saints rise to greet you with a bow.
   You wait the day saints rise to comprehend
   that we may greet and serve you here and now.

3. Attend neglected ones, the lost, the least;
   the poor, you say, approach on bending knee.
   In these you find the majesty you seek,
   and all you do for them you do for me.

From *Songs for the Cycle* © 2004 by Michael Hudson.
Church Publishing Incorporated. All rights reserved. Used by permission.

YEAR B

Meditation for Mark 13.33–37

1 Advent, Year B
"Stay awake"
66 66
Suggested tune: *Quam dilecta* or *St. Cecilia*

1. A patient presence broods
   and warms a well-placed nest,
   untroubled and alert,
   expectant and at rest.

2. She waits because she knows
   a process has begun:
   again there will be life
   before her brooding's done.

3. O nesting Spirit, praise
   to you who warm the earth
   and every longing heart
   that waits again for birth.

4. Your presence nurtures hope,
   and hope in time creates
   in us a will to bear
   the life for which we wait.

From *Songs for the Cycle* © 2004 by Michael Hudson.
Church Publishing Incorporated. All rights reserved. Used by permission.

Meditation for Mark 1.1–8

2 Advent, Year B
John the Baptist prepares the way
77 77
Suggested tune: *Bingham* or
Nun komm, der Heiden Heiland

1. When the silence takes a voice
   it may not be soft and mild:
   after years of muted peace
   words may thunder, fierce and wild.

2. John came like a storm from God,
   and a crowd was drawn to hear
   what the silence had prepared:
   "Turn to God for God is near!"

3. Near us now, though senses strain,
   strain to recognize the form
   God may take and manifest
   in the silence and the storm.

4. But our hearts search out that form,
   through the advent of the years,
   as we turn and turn again
   and again know God is near.

From *Songs for the Cycle* © 2004 by Michael Hudson.
Church Publishing Incorporated. All rights reserved. Used by permission.

Meditation for John 1.6–8, 19–28

3 Advent, Year B
John tells others about the Light
87 87
Suggested tune: *Stuttgart* or *Charlestown*
Also suitable for Epiphany

1. In the winter's early darkness,
   through the days of failing light,
   travelers may delay a journey
   or may learn to read the night.

2. Turning on a steady axis,
   cold and burning, black and bright,
   heaven tells a faithful story
   of the coming of the Light.

3. As we recognize the patterns,
   and we turn a certain way,
   even when the path is darkest
   we are faced to greet the day.

From *Songs for the Cycle* © 2004 by Michael Hudson.
Church Publishing Incorporated. All rights reserved. Used by permission.

MEDITATION FOR LUKE 1.26–38

4 Advent, Year B
Mary is visited by an angel
87 87 Double
Suggested tune: *Nettleton*

1. Countless prayers of faithful people
   weighted in a cumbrous world
   found an answer as an angel
   met an open-hearted girl.
   Not a master of a palace
   where the airs of empire swirl,
   not a young or hardened warrior
   but an open-hearted girl.

2. All the years of desperate longing
   of a people to be free
   found an eloquent expression
   in her simple, Let it be.
   Not in battle or in barter
   for a Caesar's guarantee,
   but in prayerful conversation
   and a simple, Let it be.

3. What a gift, now and whenever
   life feels barren, hope consumed,
   to recall that once a woman
   welcomed God within her womb.
   We see better now, and always,
   faith, responsive, making room,
   because once a woman, Mary,
   welcomed God within her womb.

From *Songs for the Cycle* © 2004 by Michael Hudson.
Church Publishing Incorporated. All rights reserved. Used by permission.

MEDITATION FOR JOHN 1.1–18

1 Christmas, Year B
The Word takes flesh
77 77
Suggested tune: *The Call*

1. Through the silence sounds a Word,
   deeply spoken, deeply heard.
   Life, in every realm, is stirred
   at the sounding of the Word.

2. In the darkness shines a Light,
   racing through the cosmic night.
   Ever-burning, ever-bright,
   ever-welcome is the Light.

3. Gift of God, robust and fresh,
   wakes into a simple crèche.
   Worlds, once disconnected, mesh:
   Christ, the Word and Light, takes flesh.

From *Songs for the Cycle* © 2004 by Michael Hudson.
Church Publishing Incorporated. All rights reserved. Used by permission.

MEDITATION FOR MATTHEW 2.13–15, 19–23

2 Christmas, Year B
Joseph and Mary take Jesus into Egypt
10 10 10 10
Suggested tune: *Flentge* or *Sursum Corda*

1. A family sleeps a deep, contented sleep,
   exhausted by a most amazing night.
   Rich gifts lie gathered twinkling in a heap,
   reflecting one star's fading silver light.

2. The woman leans against her husband's arm,
   her baby cradled as a mother deems;
   the three together: settled, peaceful, warm,
   until an angel stirs the father's dreams.

3. Get up! he says. Your king comes as a threat.
   Escape to Egypt while there's time enough.
   Your child is marked for struggle, but not yet—
   tonight let him know nothing else but love.

4. The parents wake, and guided by God's hand
   go into exile as their parents did,
   remembering God's promise for their land,
   relieved for now to keep the Promise hid.

From *Songs for the Cycle* © 2004 by Michael Hudson.
Church Publishing Incorporated. All rights reserved. Used by permission.

Meditation for Matthew 2.13–15, 19–23

1 Epiphany, Year B
The baptism of Jesus
66 66
Suggested tune: *St. Cecilia*

1. Let rain come down today,
   a rain to bathe the soul;
   across our wide, dry skies,
   let great, dark rain clouds roll.

2. Let streams run strong today
   to carry, fresh and clear,
   the ancient, fluid voice
   that draws a pilgrim near.

3. Let us go down today
   like Jesus did before
   to find and to pass through
   the water's open door.

From *Songs for the Cycle* © 2004 by Michael Hudson.
Church Publishing Incorporated. All rights reserved. Used by permission.

Meditation for John 1.43–51

2 Epiphany, Year B
Jesus invites others to "Come and see"
10 10 10 10
Suggested tune: *Flentge* or *Sursum Corda*

1. It was a season for a soul to wait,
   to welcome darkness like the buried corn,
   to sit with Mary through her labor pain,
   exulting in the moment God was born.

2. We stood with shepherds in a grassy field
   and tossed our twigs on their communal fire,
   exchanging stories as the midnight moon
   itself was lit by an angelic choir.

3. There was the journey through the distant hills,
   a rhythmic, mesmerizing camel ride,
   the star we learned to see through lidded eyes,
   our joy in kneeling by a baby's side.

4. How soon he grows into a force himself,
   a voice for Wisdom calling, Come and see
   the present practice of the reign of God,
   the daily wonders of Epiphany.

From *Songs for the Cycle* © 2004 by Michael Hudson.
Church Publishing Incorporated. All rights reserved. Used by permission.

Meditation for Mark 1.14–20

3 Epiphany, Year B
The continued call of the first disciples
10 10 10 10
Suggested tune: *Sursum Corda*

1 He might have stayed where John had stood before
 and waited for the world to come to him
 and been a sage that people must seek out.
 Instead he left the desert seeking them.

2 A few he found engaged beside the sea
 who did not see themselves as seekers yet.
 But soon they glimpsed a way, a truth, a life,
 they valued, did not have, could not forget.

3 And so begins the story that we tell
 and tell again, because it fosters trust
 and wonder that this spreading way of God
 has reached — and might reach farther yet through — us.

From *Songs for the Cycle* © 2004 by Michael Hudson.
Church Publishing Incorporated. All rights reserved. Used by permission.

Meditation for Mark 1.21–28

4 Epiphany, Year B
Jesus heals a demoniac in a synagogue
76 76
Suggested tune: *Ave caeli janua*

1. The Sabbath called its children,
   and one stood up to teach
   who made the ancient longings
   seem suddenly in reach.

2. A voice lashed out to counter,
   awash in animus:
   "Why should the High and Holy
   associate with us?"

3. Compassion, was the answer,
   compellingly revealed
   as this man, bruised and broken,
   was in that moment healed.

4. Then Jesus left the people,
   amazed by what they saw,
   to contemplate God's goodness
   in silence and in awe.

From *Songs for the Cycle* © 2004 by Michael Hudson.
Church Publishing Incorporated. All rights reserved. Used by permission.

Meditation for Mark 1.29–39

5 Epiphany, Year B
Jesus heals Peter's mother-in-law
LM
Suggested tune: *Puer nobis* or *The Eighth Tune*

1. The grace of God cannot be fixed
   or fastened to a sanctioned spot:
   when we move as the Spirit moves,
   there is no place where God is not.

2. We cannot tell the rain to fall
   or change the world with every prayer,
   and yet in every place we go
   the grace of God is also there —

3. To mend the broken, tend the sick,
   to share the struggles of the poor,
   to fight for justice, work for peace,
   to warn the foolish and the sure.

4. God, may we bring this consciousness
   to every circumstance we face —
   With every need you also pair
   the possibility of grace.

From *Songs for the Cycle* © 2004 by Michael Hudson.
Church Publishing Incorporated. All rights reserved. Used by permission.

Meditation for Mark 1.40–45

6 Epiphany, Year B
Jesus heals a leper and tells him to be quiet
87 87
Suggested tune: *Omni die* or *Stuttgart*

1. Silence is a way of holding
   seed from God until it roots,
   welcoming, beneath the surface,
   life to fill the rising shoots.

2. Jesus brought concern for people,
   ailing, anguished, trodden, crushed,
   and to their surprise and wonder
   often left them healed and hushed —

3. Healed of wounds and soul-abrasions
   where uncaring feet had trod;
   hushed to savor and consider,
   inwardly, the Gift of God.

4. Silence is a way of holding
   seed from God until it roots,
   welcoming, beneath the surface,
   life to fill the rising shoots.

From *Songs for the Cycle* © 2004 by Michael Hudson.
Church Publishing Incorporated. All rights reserved. Used by permission.

Meditation for Mark 2.1–12

7 Epiphany, Year B
Jesus heals a paralytic
65 65
Suggested tune: *Wem in Leidenstagen*

1. Life presents the puzzles
   Wisdom moves to solve —
   living in the balance,
   seasoned faith evolves.

2. One soul longs for meaning,
   questing every day,
   gaining in the seeking
   faith to find her way.

3. One soul keeps tradition,
   trusting truths long known,
   gaining in the keeping
   faith beyond his own.

4. Each will need the other
   in their kindred search,
   gaining in the meeting
   one enduring Church.

From *Songs for the Cycle* © 2004 by Michael Hudson.
Church Publishing Incorporated. All rights reserved. Used by permission.

Meditation for Mark 2.18–22

8 Epiphany, Year B
The wedding feast and new wineskins
11 11 11 11
Suggested tune: *St. Denio*

1. Today we are gathered to join in a feast,
   a medley of people, the outcast, the priest,
   the sinful, the lonely, the bent, and the odd,
   together we come for the marriage of God.

2. The earth celebrates with the excess of spring,
   the stars fling out silver and gold for new rings,
   the cosmos refashions immutable laws,
   as quasars and quarks flash delighted applause.

3. We bring simple gifts and stand poised to rejoice,
   to praise the Beloved, God's partner of choice.
   But praise becomes wonder — we learn it is we
   the Holy has chosen as partner-to-be.

4. So ring the bells loudly, pour into the streets
   and gather whomever you happen to meet.
   Invite and cajole them, encourage and prod —
   let none go unasked to the marriage of God.

From *Songs for the Cycle* © 2004 by Michael Hudson.
Church Publishing Incorporated. All rights reserved. Used by permission.

Meditation for Mark 9.2–9

Last Epiphany, Year B
The Mount of Transfiguration
87 87
Suggested tune: *Omni die*
(See also the text for Last Epiphany, Year A)

1. Every pilgrim has a mountain
   that is hers alone to climb,
   rising from the deepest places,
   standing through the rush of time.

2. Every mountain has a summit
   calling out to him who seeks,
   though the way is often winding
   and the summoning oblique.

3. Every summit has a threshold
   with a path from either side,
   where the hopeful meet the Hoped-for
   and the guided know their Guide.

4. Guide us now and guide us always,
   God of pilgrimage and peak,
   Source of all that draws and drives us,
   Sum of everything we seek.

From *Songs for the Cycle* © 2004 by Michael Hudson.
Church Publishing Incorporated. All rights reserved. Used by permission.

Meditation for Mark 1.9–13

1 Lent, Year B
(Especially appropriate for the service of
Ash Wednesday with imposition of ashes)
The Spirit drives Jesus into the desert
77 77
Suggested tune: *Bingham* or *Gott sei Dank*

1. Desert Wind, find us again,
   move us on to where we learn
   we are children of the dust
   and to dust we shall return.

2. Life begins with blithe intent
   and burns quick with bright desires
   but will also be revealed
   in the ashes of our fires.

3. This is Lent's epiphany —
   Wisdom deconstructing fear,
   as we see that life is short
   and yet trust that God is near.

4. Desert Wind, find us again,
   move us on to where we learn
   we are children of the dust
   and to dust we shall return.

From *Songs for the Cycle* © 2004 by Michael Hudson.
Church Publishing Incorporated. All rights reserved. Used by permission.

MEDITATION FOR MARK 8.31–38

2 Lent, Year B
Peter fails to understand Jesus' path
CMD
Suggested tune: *Kingsfold* or *Salvation*
(See also the text for Proper 17, Year A)

1 If we desire a deeper life
   then we must choose between
   the passage God proposes and
   the passage we have dreamed.
   For early dreams, though big and broad,
   meander unfulfilled
   and have no depth until God's hand
   can dredge a dreamer's silt.

2 If we desire a better world,
   then life must make its course
   in us, a river running to
   the thirsty from its Source.
   And we, as deepened channels, bless
   this water on its way,
   rejoicing that we touch and know
   the Life that we convey.

From *Songs for the Cycle* © 2004 by Michael Hudson.
Church Publishing Incorporated. All rights reserved. Used by permission.

Meditation for John 2.13–22

3 Lent, Year B
Jesus clears the Temple grounds
14 14 14 (86 86 86)
Suggested tune: *Morning Tune* or *Brother James' Air*

1. What signs will carry God today to our accustomed eyes,
   what light will penetrate the depths of knowledge crystallized,
   what voice revive a living hope made faint by its reprise?

2. When Jesus found the temple full of ritual congealed,
   he braided cords and made a whip — his passion would not yield
   to practices that covered up as much as they revealed.

3. What cords will Jesus find today to braid for our rebuff,
   what tables will be overturned, what sacrificial doves
   released, that flying free might point the path to our first love?

From *Songs for the Cycle* © 2004 by Michael Hudson.
Church Publishing Incorporated. All rights reserved. Used by permission.

Meditation for John 6.4–15

4 Lent, Year B
Jesus feeds a crowd
87 87
Suggested tune: *Omni die*

1. Jesus watched us from a mountain,
   moving toward him up the slope,
   bringing basic human hunger —
   a community of hope.

2. We were climbing with a purpose,
   bearing poverty like seed
   to be scattered on the mountain —
   a community of need.

3. Jesus gathered us in welcome,
   sat us on the grassy earth,
   paid attention to our longing —
   a community of worth.

4. Then with gifts a child presented
   Jesus saw that we were fed
   and brimful of like compassion —
   a community of bread.

From *Songs for the Cycle* © 2004 by Michael Hudson.
Church Publishing Incorporated. All rights reserved. Used by permission.

Meditation for John 12.20–33

5 Lent, Year B
Unless a seed falls in the ground and dies
44 6 D with refrain
Suggested tune: *Coventry Carol*
Also suitable for Good Friday

1. Fall to the earth, small solitary seed,
   fall to the earth today.

2. The one whose hand prepares the land
   asks you to pass this way.
   The ground is cleared, the time is near —
   fall to the earth today.

3. A gentle wind will bear you in,
   into the furrowed clay.
   The husk must break before life wakes —
   fall to the earth today.

4. Sweet is the grief that finds the leaf
   green where the brown seed lay.
   One small seed dies, uncounted rise —
   fall to the earth today.

5. Fall to the earth, small solitary seed,
   fall to the earth today.

From *Songs for the Cycle* © 2004 by Michael Hudson.
Church Publishing Incorporated. All rights reserved. Used by permission.

Meditation for Palm Sunday

Year B
Jesus enters Jerusalem
LM
Suggested tune: *Winchester New*

1. We raise our branches high today
   to sign Hosanna and to warn:
   The hands that wield a waving branch
   may also weave a crown of thorns.

2. We sing exultant songs today,
   yet singing we remember this:
   The lips that bring the sweetest praise
   may also bear the sharpest kiss.

3. We greet a golden dawn today
   and marvel as the darkness grows
   that even stalwart confidence
   may fail before the rooster crows.

4. And so our hearts are shaped today
   by palms, a kiss, a friend's denial,
   to hold the very simple prayer —
   God, save us from the time of trial.

From *Songs for the Cycle* © 2004 by Michael Hudson.
Church Publishing Incorporated. All rights reserved. Used by permission.

Meditation for Mark's Easter Narrative

Year B
Three women find the empty tomb
12 12 88
(or 66 66 44 44)
Suggested tune: *Love Unknown*

1. Three women walk alone; unquieted each communes
   with disbelief a life so full could ebb so soon.
   They seek the dead but meet instead
   the Silence of an empty tomb.

2. No stone now blocks their way; before them like a womb
   the love of God as yet unfathomed in the gloom
   invites them in to apprehend
   the Silence of an empty tomb.

3. No final rite for grief, no body to perfume,
   no parting like the tender parting they assumed.
   Their lord is gone, and life rests on
   the Silence of an empty tomb.

From *Songs for the Cycle* © 2004 by Michael Hudson.
Church Publishing Incorporated. All rights reserved. Used by permission.

Meditation for John 20.19–31

2 Easter, Years A, B, and C
Jesus appears to Thomas
10 10 10 10
Suggested tune: *Nyack*

1. I have not seen, how am I to believe?
   My eyes have never marked the risen Christ.
   Is one to trust the stories others tell,
   God raising up what has been sacrificed?

2. I have not felt his hands, stone cold, grow warm,
   nor heard that heart, once silenced, beat again,
   yet here I am, surrounded by a faith
   that apprehends his presence now as then.

3. We hope for signs, but in the end must trust
   that risen Life, arising, surely weaves
   with faith and doubt alike a living truth
   that blesses all who question to believe.

From *Songs for the Cycle* © 2004 by Michael Hudson.
Church Publishing Incorporated. All rights reserved. Used by permission.

Meditation for Luke 24.36b–48

3 Easter, Year B
The disciples encounter the risen Christ
65 65
Suggested tune: *Wem in Leidenstagen*

1. Present, though unlooked for,
   Christ comes to his friends,
   making new beginnings
   from imagined ends.

2. On a road, retreating,
   grieving for the dead,
   two engage the Living
   breaking common bread.

3. In a closed room, cloistered,
   skeptics meet the Lord
   and have in that moment
   faith and strength restored.

4. Through a dark night fishing,
   strained eyes glimpse a fire—
   it is Christ rekindling
   smoldering desire.

5. Present, though unlooked for,
   Christ comes to his friends
   making new beginnings
   from imagined ends.

From *Songs for the Cycle* © 2004 by Michael Hudson.
Church Publishing Incorporated. All rights reserved. Used by permission.

Meditation for John 10.11–16

4 Easter, Year B
Jesus the Good Shepherd
(Especially suitable for children)
87 87 77
Suggested tune: *Irby*

1. David was a daring shepherd
   long before he was a king,
   besting lions and bears in battle,
   armed with sticks and stones and sling.
   Strong, resourceful, ruddy-cheeked,
   David grew up tending sheep.

2. Jesus also was a shepherd —
   people were his constant care.
   And he also battled danger,
   more than wolves or lions or bears.
   He fought anything at all
   that made God's great love seem small.

3. We can grow up strong like David,
   we can love like Jesus, too,
   joining hands with God the Shepherd
   tending all that's just and true
   till the whole world, wide and deep,
   makes a place for all God's sheep.

From *Songs for the Cycle* © 2004 by Michael Hudson.
Church Publishing Incorporated. All rights reserved. Used by permission.

Meditation for John 14.15–21

5 Easter, Year B
Jesus promises the Spirit
CM
Suggested tune: *Detroit*

1. There is a song the Spirit sings,
   it lodges in the heart
   and throbs deep down the soul of things,
   a constant counterpart.

2. We hear it like a storm through trees
   and stand aware and braced
   to meet it. Ah, it comes, a breeze
   felt fresh upon the face.

3. We follow where the music leads,
   or try and fall behind,
   recovering the melody
   in each small note we find.

4. Sing on, Creating Spirit, sing,
   our listening spirits long
   to study all that sparks and springs
   created in your song.

From *Songs for the Cycle* © 2004 by Michael Hudson.
Church Publishing Incorporated. All rights reserved. Used by permission.

Meditation for John 15.9–17

6 Easter, Year B
Love one another as I have loved you
87 87 87 refrain
Suggested tune: *Divinum mysterium*
(equal note value)

1. From a time beyond beginnings
   when all worlds were yet unformed,
   through the fire of first creation
   when our atoms swirled and swarmed,
   through the cooling of the planets
   long before a heart was warmed—
   We are loved. Ah, we are loved.

2. From the deep and wordless longings
   of the primal waking soul,
   through the years of fluent conscience
   when the prophets' thunder rolled,
   to the days when Jesus' wisdom
   wove our remnant spirits whole—
   We are loved. Ah, we are loved.

3. From today's unfolding moments
   rounding from the recent night,
   through the sum of all tomorrows
   rising dim or breaking bright,
   to the point where every ending
   gathers into endless light—
   We are loved. Ah, we are loved.

From *Songs for the Cycle* © 2004 by Michael Hudson.
Church Publishing Incorporated. All rights reserved. Used by permission.

Meditation for John 17.11b–19

7 Easter, Year B
Ministry amid danger
87 87
Suggested tune: *Restoration*

1. In the comfort that we cling to
   in the brittle, failing light
   we find boldness that persuades us
   to take fire into the night.

2. In the great love that through deluge
   holds us close and keeps us warm
   we find passion that compels us
   to take peace into the storm.

3. In the purpose that sustains us
   as we soar and as we plod
   we find grace to ferry others
   on the rising wind of God.

From *Songs for the Cycle* © 2004 by Michael Hudson.
Church Publishing Incorporated. All rights reserved. Used by permission.

A Meditation for Pentecost

Pentecost, Year B
Encountering Spirit
11 11 13 11
Suggested tune: *Adoro devote*
(3rd line — 1 note = 1 syllable)
(See also the text for Pentecost, Year A)

1. To the edge of oceans where waves engage stone
   many make their journeys, allied or alone,
   seeking out the space between the firm ground and the sea
   where the ancient hinges moor a mystery.

2. To the edge of mountains where the view is wide
   many climb to witness earth and sky collide,
   seeking Jacob's double stair or Sarah's sacred oak,
   yearning for the showings such a place evokes.

3. To the edge of meaning where the soul is stilled,
   and the certain emptied, and the empty filled,
   here the Spirit brings us day and night and night and day,
   here where faith and knowing meet and mark our Way.

From *Songs for the Cycle* © 2004 by Michael Hudson.
Church Publishing Incorporated. All rights reserved. Used by permission.

A Meditation Suitable for Trinity Sunday

Long Meter
Suggested tune: *Conditor alme siderum*
or *The Eighth Tune*

1. A narrow door need not exclude
   one soul who turns to God today,
   but opens to reveal the link
   between the near and faraway.

2. As windows in the circled stones
   convey a single shaft of light
   to strike and mark the crucial point,
   a narrow door puts God in sight.

3. And if we have to change our course
   or climb or bend and sometimes strain
   to catch the light, a child of God
   will know it as creative pain.

4. O God, our Source and Goal and Guide,
   the Ground we know and yet explore,
   you draw us to this opening
   and meet us in the narrow door.

From *Songs for the Cycle* © 2004 by Michael Hudson.
Church Publishing Incorporated. All rights reserved. Used by permission.

Meditation for Mark 2.23–28

Proper 4, Year B
Jesus breaks a Sabbath tradition
CM
Suggested tune: *Dundee*

1. The Church's lasting paradox,
   our challenge every day —
   to keep and to communicate
   the narrative of faith —

2. The story of God's life with us
   in Sacrament and Word,
   the many treasures handed down
   and faithfully preserved.

3. As stewards of the Mystery
   our hold will not be tight,
   a dusty vault, a heavy lid
   will only block its light.

4. The task invigorates the soul
   and focuses the day —
   to guard the gracious gifts of God
   while giving them away.

From *Songs for the Cycle* © 2004 by Michael Hudson.
Church Publishing Incorporated. All rights reserved. Used by permission.

MEDITATION FOR LUKE 7.1–10

Proper 5, Year B
Jesus is accused of being possessed
CM
Suggested tune: *Irish*

1. A loving heart cannot keep still
   when friends are in great need —
   for love, twined as it is with God,
   exists to intercede.

2. A hopeful heart conspires with God
   and dreams and acts. Or waits.
   And opens to the branching paths
   that hopefulness creates.

3. A vital heart cannot abide
   a dank, unwholesome space —
   We see how Christ infused the world
   with energy and grace.

4. God, give us energy to face
   a needful world wide-eyed
   and step each day into the breach
   where love and need collide.

From *Songs for the Cycle* © 2004 by Michael Hudson.
Church Publishing Incorporated. All rights reserved. Used by permission.

Meditation for Mark 4.26–34

Proper 6, Year B
The principle of growth in the Realm of God
LM
Suggested tune: *Conditor alme siderum*

1. There is a goodness in the ground,
   a generosity of earth;
   a forest shows it in the seed
   that sleeps and springs to summer birth.

2. There is a spark shot through our core,
   a strong, compassion-lit desire;
   we see it as the Breath of God
   sweeps by to brighten us like fire.

3. God fits a blessing in all things —
   through all the world we see and know,
   there is the wonderful intent
   to warm and wake, to live and grow!

From *Songs for the Cycle* © 2004 by Michael Hudson.
Church Publishing Incorporated. All rights reserved. Used by permission.

Meditation for Mark 4.35–41 (5.1–20)

Proper 7, Year B
Jesus calms a storm and heals a man with demons
87 87 D
Suggested tune: *Holy Manna*

1. There's a land across the water,
though the sea is deep and wide
and a storm disturbs the crossing,
we can reach the other side.
There's a boat to carry Jesus,
and a host of boats beside
set to bear up all believers
on a rising, wind-stirred tide.

2. And when waves worry the water
and dark clouds begin to form,
we can trust a mighty Spirit,
near to still the fiercest storm.
God desires that we cross over
and empowers arm and oar—
there are many needful people
waiting on the farther shore.

3. We will reach the coast of heaven
on some other, distant day.
For today, we sail with Jesus
and help others on the way
to that land across the water,
though the sea is deep and wide,
and a storm disturbs the crossing,
we can reach the other side.

From *Songs for the Cycle* © 2004 by Michael Hudson.
Church Publishing Incorporated. All rights reserved. Used by permission.

Meditation for Mark 5.22–24, 35b–43

Proper 8, Year B
Jesus returns Jairus' daughter to life
10 10 11 11
Suggested tune: *Laudate Dominum*
(See also the text for Proper 5, Year C)

1. God's love, like a stream born high in green hills,
   springs fresh and rolls on, calls loudly and spills
   its life-making wetness across a wide earth,
   and spreads to all creatures continuing birth.

2. Our thirst, like a root thrust down through the ground,
   turns to and attends the river's rich sound.
   We grow towards God's goodness, like all things, we know
   to seek out the places where deep waters flow.

3. Praise God for the stream that springs from the hills,
   and God for the roots the vast river fills,
   and God for this blessing of water and thirst —
   may we in God's graciousness all be immersed.

From *Songs for the Cycle* © 2004 by Michael Hudson.
Church Publishing Incorporated. All rights reserved. Used by permission.

Meditation for Mark 6.1–6

Proper 9, Year B
Jesus returns home and is lightly regarded
87 87
Suggested tune: *Halton Holgate*

1. Hidden in the ordinary,
   unobserved in plain disguise,
   God prepares a revelation
   and awaits, a rich surprise!

2. Jesus, newly known as healer,
   teacher, prophet, chosen-One,
   journeyed home where people named him
   brother, cousin, neighbor, son.

3. God strews flowers through the desert,
   paints a dawn in unwatched skies
   and unfolds the Incarnation
   right before unseeing eyes.

4. May our spirits be attentive,
   eager as we breathe the prayer:
   God, may we perceive you, present,
   every day and everywhere.

From *Songs for the Cycle* © 2004 by Michael Hudson.
Church Publishing Incorporated. All rights reserved. Used by permission.

Meditation for Mark 6.7–13

Proper 10, Year B
Jesus sends out disciples
11 11 11 11
Suggested tune: *Cradle Song*
(See also the text for Proper 9, Year C)

1. A road at our doorstep, a light in the sky,
   a point in the distance that catches the eye,
   a sense of the possible, fresh in the air —
   we know God has given us something to share.

2. We set out with little, no money or bread,
   few cumbersome comforts or burdens; instead,
   we wish to walk lightly, to go with Godspeed,
   to follow the prompting wherever it leads.

3. The road takes us places we never have been
   and moves us towards others, a circle of friends
   who need what we offer — and also who yearn
   to offer us something we need in return.

4. And this is the journey, God's gifts spread among
   all manner of people, community sprung
   in kindness, compassion, in simple good deeds —
   the mutual meeting of gifts and of needs.

From *Songs for the Cycle* © 2004 by Michael Hudson.
Church Publishing Incorporated. All rights reserved. Used by permission.

Meditation for Mark 6.30–44

Proper 11, Year B
Jesus feeds a crowd
11 11 10 11
Suggested tune: *Noël nouvelet*

1. Taking what is given, small as it may seem,
   scant or insufficient, still we dare to dream —
   small can make much, when gathered in God's love,
   and our simple gifts may prove to be enough.

2. Blessing what is given, small as it may seem,
   scant or insufficient, still we dare to dream —
   small can make much, rejoicing in God's love,
   and our simple gifts may prove to be enough.

3. Sharing what is given, small as it may seem,
   scant or insufficient, still we dare to dream —
   small can make much, when offered in God's love,
   and our simple gifts may prove to be enough.

From *Songs for the Cycle* © 2004 by Michael Hudson.
Church Publishing Incorporated. All rights reserved. Used by permission.

Meditation for Mark 6.45–52

Proper 12, Year B
Jesus comes to his disciples across the water
LM
Suggested tune: *Danby*

1. Into the night Christ sent his friends,
   against the wind and stinging spray;
   they fought a restless sea while he
   climbed deep into the hills to pray.

2. Alone at last with God in prayer,
   immersed in rich, renewing peace,
   Christ turned again to find his friends
   and strode to them across the sea.

3. He came beyond all common sense,
   like God to prophet, passing by,
   seen and not seen, known yet unknown.
   And then he told them, "It is I."

4. The wind fell slack, the sea stood still,
   the stars wheeled round remembered skies;
   and Jesus climbed into the boat,
   familiar and unrecognized.

From *Songs for the Cycle* © 2004 by Michael Hudson.
Church Publishing Incorporated. All rights reserved. Used by permission.

Meditation for John 6.24–35

Proper 13, Year B
"I am the Bread of Life"
11 11 11 5
Suggested tune: *Caelites plaudant*

1. New every morning is our human yearning.
   Safety and shelter, nurture and belonging,
   wholeness and meaning is the bread we hope for
   morning by morning.

2. Fresh as the dewfall, beaded in the sunlight,
   sprinkled like manna waiting to be gathered,
   Christ is our longing and our brimming over,
   new every morning.

From *Songs for the Cycle* © 2004 by Michael Hudson.
Church Publishing Incorporated. All rights reserved. Used by permission.

Meditation for John 6.37–51

Proper 14, Year B
"I am the Bread of Life"...continued
10 10 10 10
Suggested tune: *Slane*
(See also the text for Proper 9, Year B)

1. Blessed is the hunger that lifts up the head,
   turns us toward home where a table is spread,
   daily reminds us to come and be fed,
   blessed is the hunger that lifts up the head.

2. Blessed is the passion that brightens the eyes,
   scans the horizon for each day's surprise,
   welcomes the messengers who make us wise,
   blessed is the passion that brightens the eyes.

3. Blessed is the path that is marked and well-trod,
   smoothed by the numberless pilgrims who plod
   on toward the prodigal welcome of God,
   blessed is the path that is marked and well-trod.

4. Blessed are the friends that we meet on the way,
   old friends and new friends, the young and the gray,
   those who must leave us and those who will stay,
   blessed are the friends that we meet on the way.

5. Blessed is the table we gather around,
   ample and anchored on peaceable ground,
   center and sign of the Bread we have found,
   blessed is the table we gather around.

From *Songs for the Cycle* © 2004 by Michael Hudson.
Church Publishing Incorporated. All rights reserved. Used by permission.

Meditation for John 6.53–59

Proper 15, Year B
"Those who eat my flesh and drink my blood abide in me"
10 10 10 10
Suggested tune: *Sursum Corda*

1. The gifts we have presented move toward God.
   Our small and ever-hopeful offerings
   are gathered, blessed, and lifted up as we
   consider and encounter holy things.

2. We wait, and bread is placed within our hand.
   We note the taste of wine upon the tongue
   and marvel, that in meeting holy things,
   we somehow meet and know a holy One.

3. And as we are attentive in this time,
   we find the meal we take, the One we bless
   is blessing and is also taking us
   and making of us gifts of holiness.

From *Songs for the Cycle* © 2004 by Michael Hudson.
Church Publishing Incorporated. All rights reserved. Used by permission.

Meditation for John 6.60–69

Proper 16, Year B
"To whom would we go?
You have the words of eternal life"
66 66
Suggested tune: *Quam dilecta*

1 You have the words of life.
  We have a heart to hear,
  a mind to know, a will
  to turn a listening ear.

2 You have the words of life,
  a beating, breathing creed
  that fires a conscious quest
  and fills a depthless need.

3 You have the words of life.
  We feed on what you say,
  and, having tasted well,
  we will not turn away.

From *Songs for the Cycle* © 2004 by Michael Hudson.
Church Publishing Incorporated. All rights reserved. Used by permission.

Meditation for Mark 7.1–8, 14–15, 21–23

Proper 17, Year B
"You abandon the commandment of God
and hold to human tradition"
CM
Suggested tune: *Dundee*

1. The Church's lasting paradox,
   our challenge every day —
   to keep and to communicate
   the narrative of faith…

2. The story of God's life with us
   in Sacrament and Word,
   the many treasures handed down
   and faithfully preserved.

3. As stewards of the Mystery
   our hold will not be tight,
   a dusty vault, a heavy lid
   will only block its light.

4. The task invigorates the soul
   and focuses the day —
   to guard the gracious gifts of God
   while giving them away.

From *Songs for the Cycle* © 2004 by Michael Hudson.
Church Publishing Incorporated. All rights reserved. Used by permission.

Meditation for Mark 7.31–37

Proper 18, Year B
Jesus shows compassion to a "foreigner"
77 77
Suggested tune: *Nun komm, der Heiden Heiland*

1. Fishers fishing not for fish
   learned to welcome all they met
   watching Jesus stitch a world
   into one connective net...

2. Helping float the supple cords
   north and east and south and west,
   reaching through long tides and times
   friend and kin and all the rest...

3. Neighbor, stranger, wounded, well,
   Roman, Hebrew, slave, and free,
   landless, homeless, well-to-do,
   dark-skinned, light-skinned, you and me.

4. Praise the fishers, praise the net,
   praise the interlacing strands,
   praise the wildly varied catch
   gathered into God's strong hands.

From *Songs for the Cycle* © 2004 by Michael Hudson.
Church Publishing Incorporated. All rights reserved. Used by permission.

Meditation for Mark 8.27–38

Proper 19, Year B
Misunderstanding the way of the cross,
Peter rebukes Jesus
10 10 10 10
Suggested tune: *Sursum Corda*

1. The way to Life takes unexpected turns,
   contrary to what one anticipates.
   Who plots a path through hell's uneasy streets
   to reach the peace of heaven's sturdy gates?

2. We meet the warm, transforming love of God,
   embrace and praise it, yet misunderstand
   that love, to reach and warm a wider world,
   flows often crosswise to the ways we've planned.

3. Our peace in pieces lies before our eyes—
   one piece runs with and one against the grain.
   These meet and point to heaven when we bind
   God's great love in us to the world's great pain.

From *Songs for the Cycle* © 2004 by Michael Hudson.
Church Publishing Incorporated. All rights reserved. Used by permission.

MEDITATION FOR MARK 9.30–37

Proper 20, Year B
"Whoever receives one such child receives me"
44 44 D
Suggested tune: *Deirdre* (3/2 with even, not dotted rhythms)
*(stanza 6 of "I bind unto myself today")
(See also the text for Proper 9, Year A)

1. In the tangle
of our living
when the purpose
is forgotten,
we find Wisdom
quick and nimble
in the questions
of our children.

2. In the wreckage
of our battles
where the powers
have collided,
we find greatness
shyly hiding
in the frailty
of our children.

3. In the sharpness
of our actions
when compassion
is diminished,
we find mercy
deep and brimming
in the kindness
of our children.

4. In the dryness
of our being
where the sacred
has retreated,
we find Jesus
bright and bodied
in the presence
of our children.

From *Songs for the Cycle* © 2004 by Michael Hudson.
Church Publishing Incorporated. All rights reserved. Used by permission.

Meditation for Mark 9.38–48

Proper 21, Year B
"Whoever is not against us is for us"
88 77
(one syllable to one note in lines 1 and 2)
Suggested tune: *The Call*

1. Bless the good wherever it grows,
   bless whatever gardener sows
   seed to turn the bare ground green
   through an Earth where all may glean.

2. Bless the truth wherever it blooms;
   in God's house are numerous rooms.
   Let a thousand colors grace
   sill and table, urn and vase.

3. Bless the fair wherever it shines,
   every star and atom that signs
   God above us, ice and fire,
   God within us, heart's desire.

From *Songs for the Cycle* © 2004 by Michael Hudson.
Church Publishing Incorporated. All rights reserved. Used by permission.

Meditation for Mark 10.2–9

Proper 22, Year B
What God has joined together
10 10 10 10
Suggested tune: *Slane*

1. Love is a longing, a flame in the night
   drawing us singly to link and unite,
   lighting the promise we have at the start —
   God in the pairing of each longing heart.

2. Love is a tether, the reason we stay
   one with another through difficult days,
   learning to savor in bright times and tears
   God in the friendship that comes with the years.

3. Love is a wounding, a deepening scar
   burned by the fire of our own nearest star,
   searing our spirits so we might contain
   God in the getting and healing of pain.

4. Love is a treasure, a gift to the soul —
   by it the Giver woos us to be whole,
   through it we find, in our failings and arts,
   God in the other we hold in our hearts.

From *Songs for the Cycle* © 2004 by Michael Hudson.
Church Publishing Incorporated. All rights reserved. Used by permission.

Meditation for Mark 10.17–27

Proper 23, Year B
"Give all that you have to the poor,
and come follow me"
77 77
Suggested tune: *Bingham*
(See also the text for 2 Epiphany Year A)

1. Brother Sun and Sister Moon,
   spilling light as you slip by,
   you and we forever are
   siblings in the starry sky.

2. Flashing fish and sleeping bear,
   humming bee and nesting bird,
   you and we are ever borne
   by the same Creative Word.

3. Fern and willow, leaf and root,
   stream and ocean, rock and sand,
   you and we are ever held
   in the same Sustaining Hand.

4. All we creatures, great and small,
   are the heirs of sacred wealth,
   and we all, together, live
   by the other's Lasting Health.

5. God of saint and God of snail,
   God of forest, earth, and air,
   may we grow to love you well
   in the Common Life we share.

This text is a stretch as a meditation on the wealthy seeker. Yet in reading this as a text that falls in the Creation Cycle and that is based on the gospel of a wealthy but ambivalent seeker, perhaps we as human members of the larger family of God might choose to consider ways of seeking and serving Christ that do not impoverish our "brothers and sisters" in the whole of creation.

From *Songs for the Cycle* © 2004 by Michael Hudson.
Church Publishing Incorporated. All rights reserved. Used by permission.

Meditation for Mark 10.35–45

Proper 24, Year B
The Son of Man came not to be served but to serve
77 77
Suggested tune: *Gott sei Dank*
or *Aus der Tiefe rufe ich*

1. Wisdom makes a way to God
   that the shrewd are slow to take,
   where the kingdom of a self
   dwindles for compassion's sake.

2. Greatness builds a house for God
   that the great sometimes ignore,
   where a single passageway
   opens through a servants' door.

3. Power shapes a realm of God
   that the powerful confound,
   where the dominant is dimmed
   and the dominated crowned.

4. Gracious, potent, pliant Christ,
   may we followers observe
   that through you God's greatness moves
   not to master but to serve.

From *Songs for the Cycle* © 2004 by Michael Hudson.
Church Publishing Incorporated. All rights reserved. Used by permission.

Meditation for Mark 10.46–52

Proper 25, Year B
Blind Bartimaeus calls out to be healed
11 11 11 5
Suggested tune: *Bickford*
(See also the text for 4 Lent, Year A)

1. Sightless and useless in the eyes of many,
   pushed to the edges of a people's notice,
   one yet has courage, and will not keep silent,
   calling to Jesus.

2. Hearing the one cry raised above the many,
   sensing a quick soul slowed by the unseeing,
   bearing compassion and the hope of wholeness,
   Jesus comes nearer.

3. Touched by God's goodness, one among the many
   gains understanding and the gift of vision,
   and with a wide world bright and undiscovered,
   one follows Jesus.

*From Songs for the Cycle © 2004 by Michael Hudson.
Church Publishing Incorporated. All rights reserved. Used by permission.*

Meditation for Mark 12.28–34

Proper 26, Year B
Love for God and others
98 88
Suggested tune: *Tender Thought*

1. God, I would love you with all my heart,
   my mind, my soul, my joy, my tears;
   though you exist beyond all loves,
   still love desires to love you here.

2. Here we will find you in every heart
   that beats and bleeds and cries for peace,
   and love you well by loving them
   until the cries and bleeding cease.

3. Ceaseless the restlessness of our hearts
   to reach the depth for which we delve,
   and find this Love Beyond All Loves
   and love all others as ourselves.

From *Songs for the Cycle* © 2004 by Michael Hudson.
Church Publishing Incorporated. All rights reserved. Used by permission.

Meditation for Mark 12.38–44

Proper 27, Year B
The widow's generous gift
87 87
Suggested tune: *Omni die*

1. Simple gifts of faithful people
splashed like raindrops on the sand,
one by one and all together
spread refreshment through a land.

2. Willing hands of mindful people
linked and pressing palm to palm,
like a reef around an island,
still the waves and aid the calm.

3. Liberal love of caring people,
given both to foes and friends,
makes in time the sea of difference
that the grace of God intends.

From *Songs for the Cycle* © 2004 by Michael Hudson.
Church Publishing Incorporated. All rights reserved. Used by permission.

Meditation for Mark 13.14–23

Proper 28, Year B
A warning about impending doom
LM
Suggested tune: *Dickinson College*

1. When apprehension frets the soul
   and banished demons reappear,
   we find serenity again
   remembering love casts out fear.

2. When sly misgivings bar our way
   and all paths forward seem unclear,
   we find the courage to walk on
   remembering love casts out fear.

3. When hope feels scattered to the stars
   and thoughts of light will not cohere,
   we find the Center we forget
   remembering love casts out fear.

From *Songs for the Cycle* © 2004 by Michael Hudson.
Church Publishing Incorporated. All rights reserved. Used by permission.

Meditation for Last Pentecost

Proper 29, Year B
Christ the King
10 10 10 10
Suggested tune: *Flentge*
(See also the text for Proper 29, Year C)

1   O Jesus, we have tried to make you King
    and hoped for crowns on earth and thrones above,
    but you resist triumphalistic dreams
    and bring instead a majesty of love.

2   We wait the day when "Christ the King" descends
    and all saints rise to greet you with a bow.
    You wait the day saints rise to comprehend
    that we may greet and serve you here and now.

3   Attend neglected ones, the lost, the least;
    the poor, you say, approach on bending knee.
    In these you find the majesty you seek,
    and all you do for them you do for me.

From *Songs for the Cycle* © 2004 by Michael Hudson.
Church Publishing Incorporated. All rights reserved. Used by permission.

YEAR C

Meditation for Luke 21.25–31

1 Advent, Year C
Signs of the end
87 87
Suggested tune: *Omni die* or *Stuttgart*

1. Though the fig tree does not blossom
   and the spring brings fire and snow,
   still will I hope for a future
   where the fruit of God yet grows.

2. Though the oceans seethe and threaten
   and the waves tear at the land,
   still will I pray for a future
   where the oaks of God yet stand.

3. Though the sun sets cold and sullen
   and the moon comes dull and red,
   still will I trust in a future
   where the light of God yet spreads.

4. Though the cities surge with chaos
   and appalling deeds are dared,
   still will I look for a future
   where the peace of God is shared.

5. Though the nations clash and wrangle
   and religions spar and strive,
   still will I work for a future
   where the love of God yet thrives.

From *Songs for the Cycle* © 2004 by Michael Hudson.
Church Publishing Incorporated. All rights reserved. Used by permission.

MEDITATION FOR LUKE 3.1–6

2 Advent, Year C
Prepare the way
77 77
Suggested tune: *Aus der Tiefe rufe ich*

1. Change sleeps deeply as the child
forming in its mother's womb;
rhythms ancient as the sea
soothe today but startle soon.

2. Change burns slowly as a fire
smoored to last the bitter night;
ashes deep and soft as snow
cloak but do not quench its light.

3. Change flies quietly as a hawk
soaring in a winter sky;
with an easy tilt of wing
miles of fallow ground sweep by.

4. Change wakes swiftly as a storm
boiling in the desert air;
mindful people mark its rise
and determine to prepare.

From *Songs for the Cycle* © 2004 by Michael Hudson.
Church Publishing Incorporated. All rights reserved. Used by permission.

MEDITATION FOR LUKE 3.7–18

3 Advent, Year C
John speaks of practical righteousness
and of the One who is to come
SM
Suggested tune: Franconia

1. Do what you know to do
   today and everyday,
   and know that One is coming soon
   to clarify the way.

2. Share gladly what you have
   with those who live with less,
   and know that One is coming soon
   who blesses graciousness.

3. Let justice be the star
   that steers you through the night,
   and know that One is coming soon
   who prizes what is right.

4. Sustain your heart's deep fire
   through dull and lightless days,
   for One works even now through you
   to set the world ablaze.

From *Songs for the Cycle* © 2004 by Michael Hudson.
Church Publishing Incorporated. All rights reserved. Used by permission.

Meditation for Luke 1.39–56

4 Advent, Year C
Mary visits Elizabeth
88 88
Suggested tune: *The Eighth Tune*
or *Winchester New*

1. We celebrate the openness
   of Mary and Elizabeth,
   receptive to the pulse of God
   in its presenting genesis.

2. We marvel at the readiness
   of Mary and Elizabeth
   to bear the swelling grace of God
   and its imposing holiness.

3. We wonder at the fearlessness
   of Mary and Elizabeth
   to countenance the light of God
   with such complete uncloudedness.

4. We venerate the willingness
   of Mary and Elizabeth
   to open to the gift of God
   with energy and mindfulness.

From *Songs for the Cycle* © 2004 by Michael Hudson.
Church Publishing Incorporated. All rights reserved. Used by permission.

Meditation for the Sunday after Christmas

Year C
Christ is born
Common Meter Double
Suggested tune: *Kingsfold* or *Halifax*

1. Beneath a dark, familiar sky
   the silent air was stirred;
   a sudden rush like many wings
   announced a startling word:
   a word more distant than the stars
   above the stony ground
   and closer than the beating hearts
   that marked the sudden sound.

2. The shepherds rose to face the sky,
   then turned and fell face down;
   this night it seemed that Life itself
   was pressing toward the ground
   to take, to hold, to celebrate
   the substance of the earth
   and gather all creation in
   a reconciling birth.

3. The stars aligned to point a path;
   the shepherds rose and ran,
   swept up in an epiphany
   they longed to understand.
   This longing also gathers us
   to rise and go with them,
   and find our way among the ways
   that meet in Bethlehem.

From *Songs for the Cycle* © 2004 by Michael Hudson.
Church Publishing Incorporated. All rights reserved. Used by permission.

Meditation for Matthew 2.1–12

2 Christmas, Year C
Journey of the Magi
Long Meter
Suggested tune: *The Eighth Tune*
or *Winchester New*

1. God gave a star to guide the wise,
   whose hearts were open to its light;
   to follow they gave up the day
   and went as pilgrims through the night.

2. God gave the wise to praise a child,
   who lay, a secret hope, in hay;
   the wise ones worshiped openly
   then journeyed home another way.

3. God gave the child to love a world
   that noticed neither child nor light;
   but love grew up, a brighter star,
   to guide a pilgrim through the night.

From *Songs for the Cycle* © 2004 by Michael Hudson.
Church Publishing Incorporated. All rights reserved. Used by permission.

Meditation for Luke 3

1 Epiphany, Year C
The Spirit descends on Jesus as he is baptized by John
87 87
Suggested tune: *Omni die* or *Restoration*

1. Something stirs when heaven opens,
   sweeping, birdlike, toward the land.
   Something moves to make a dwelling
   in an outstretched, upturned hand—

2. That which animates beginnings,
   brooding over sea and mud,
   and which nurtures re-creation,
   angel of the ending flood,

3. Soaring over wave and mountain,
   circling where the waters sing,
   swooping near the desert river,
   rushing toward the Fisher King.

4. Brooding, soaring, rushing Spirit,
   as we trace your forward flight,
   may our hands reach out, a dwelling
   where a migrant bird may light.

From *Songs for the Cycle* © 2004 by Michael Hudson.
Church Publishing Incorporated. All rights reserved. Used by permission.

Meditation for John 2.1–11

2 Epiphany, Year C
The wedding at Cana
10 10 10 with alleluia
Suggested tune: *Engelberg*

1 When simple mirth and joyfulness decline,
by sacred narrative we call to mind
a day when Christ changed water into wine,
Alleluia!

2 When feast and celebration are maligned,
by solemn utterance we call to mind
a day when Christ changed water into wine,
Alleluia!

3 When laughter fades and humor is confined,
in righteous company we call to mind
a day when Christ changed water into wine,
Alleluia!

4 When saints and levity are unaligned,
advised and penitent we call to mind
a day when Christ changed water into wine,
Alleluia!

From *Songs for the Cycle* © 2004 by Michael Hudson.
Church Publishing Incorporated. All rights reserved. Used by permission.

Meditation for Luke 4.14–21

3 Epiphany, Year C
Jesus defines his mission
12 10 12 10 12
Suggested tune: *Lytlington*

Christ, be now the voice that heartens the impoverished;
Christ, be now the strength that aids the anguished;
Christ, be now the sight that orients the sightless;
Christ, be now the iron that breaks oppression;
Christ, be now the song we sing of God's compassion.

From *Songs for the Cycle* © 2004 by Michael Hudson.
Church Publishing Incorporated. All rights reserved. Used by permission.

Meditation for Luke 4.21–32

4 Epiphany, Year C
Nazareth is confronted with the scope of Jesus' mission
11 10 11 10
Suggested tune: *Charterhouse*

1. Rain often falls across the distant mountains,
   though we may never climb them to explore,
   we see the greening of their slopes through summer
   and drink from rivers running near our door.

2. Snow swirls and sifts through tightly bordered branches
   to whiten all a forest world below;
   the smallest twig, each fallen leaf and needle
   bears witness to the thoroughness of snow.

3. Life surely teems on some enchanted planet
   awash in wetness and baptized by light —
   How many eyes are now regarding heaven
   from different places in the starry (starry)* night?

4. How far God's love extends to fill creation.
   How thoroughly God's peace and justice sift.
   How charged with awe and wonder is the creature
   who but begins to comprehend the gift.

*The extra two syllables work well with *Charterhouse*.

From *Songs for the Cycle* © 2004 by Michael Hudson.
Church Publishing Incorporated. All rights reserved. Used by permission.

Meditation for Luke 5.1–11

5 Epiphany, Year C
Peter's miraculous catch
CM
Suggested tune: *Dundee* or *St. Flavian*

1. A prayer can ride a breath, exhaled,
   like ashes ride a breeze
   and take away by scrap and whit
   a frazzled heart's unease.

2. There comes a time to clear a soul's
   accumulating mess,
   to trade a trove of bother for
   the gift of emptiness.

3. When Peter was a fisherman
   he found, for all his skill,
   it's often not the brimming boat
   Christ purposes to fill.

4. God, give us breath that carries off
   the refuse of the day
   and finds our lightened, anchored souls
   uncluttered as we pray.

From *Songs for the Cycle* © 2004 by Michael Hudson.
Church Publishing Incorporated. All rights reserved. Used by permission.

Meditation for Luke 6.17–26

6 Epiphany, Year C
Blessings and woes
10 10 10 6
Suggested tune: *Faith*

1. Blessed are we poor, for it is God's desire
   that we will one day tend a pleasant land —
   that all who long for sustenance might eat
   from God's incarnate hand.

2. Blessed are we grieved, whose tears roll down as prayer,
   and we maligned for God and justice' sake —
   a time will come when scorn and sorrow sleep
   and peace and laughter wake.

3. Cursed are we rich who hoard our blessings now
   and we, the full, our surfeit sloughed and hilled —
   Carve this in stone, the gifts that go unshared
   leave rifts that are not filled.

4. Cursed are we glib, whose careless laughter pains
   the pained, the bound, the strange, the dispossessed —
   may we, instead, in time extend God's joy
   that many may be blessed.

From *Songs for the Cycle* © 2004 by Michael Hudson.
Church Publishing Incorporated. All rights reserved. Used by permission.

Meditation for Luke 6.27–38

7 Epiphany, Year C
Jesus offers strategies for creatively engaging
those who oppose us
11 11 11 5
Suggested tune: *Bickford*

1. Time rounds with choices, varied and surprising.
   Through all the puzzles common life occasions
   we sense God's blessing, present as a process —
   love seeking wisdom.

2. Christ is the pattern, agile and creative,
   lithe as a dancer, partnered with dilemma.
   Over and over we see in the movement
   love seeking wisdom.

3. Tested by questions set to snare a teacher,
   greeted with smugness meant to curb compassion,
   Christ brings an answer that will teach forever —
   love seeking wisdom.

4. Give us, Creator, agile minds for thinking,
   hearts of compassion centered and outreaching,
   that in our movement others may encounter
   love seeking wisdom.

From *Songs for the Cycle* © 2004 by Michael Hudson.
Church Publishing Incorporated. All rights reserved. Used by permission.

Meditation for Luke 6.39–49

8 Epiphany, Year C
Can the blind lead the blind?
87 87 Double
Suggested tune: *Nettleton*

1. Darkness lay upon the waters,
and the starless heavens swirled
as the formless earth awaited
the creating of a world.
Over all the Spirit brooded
like a patient mother bird
for the leaping of the morning
at the speaking of a Word.

2. In another age of darkness
children stumbled, blind from birth,
as the Word of God, incarnate,
moved again upon the earth
with the re-creating promise
that the sightless would be healed
and perceive the new creation
that the light of God revealed.

3. Every soul will sit with darkness,
every eye will long for light,
every heart will lose direction
in the swirling, starless night.
Still the One who speaks the morning
moves beside us on the way;
knowing this we know that darkness
always holds the hope of day.

From *Songs for the Cycle* © 2004 by Michael Hudson.
Church Publishing Incorporated. All rights reserved. Used by permission.

Meditation for Luke 9.28–36

Last Epiphany, Year C
Transfiguration
10 9 10 9 D (1 note=1 syllable)
Suggested tune: *Pleading Savior*

1. Sometimes we come to the soul's high places,
   groping or led by a wiser hand,
   taken beyond our familiar limits,
   witnessing more than we understand.
   Singular insights spring up unsummoned,
   torah and story find form and flesh,
   hope rises up and soars unencumbered
   here where the bound and the Boundless mesh.

2. Breached are the walls of the fixed and patterned,
   burst are the banks that divert the flood,
   in streams the tide of the gleaming Spirit
   lighting the earth with its bright lifeblood.
   Even the ground where, kneeling, we settle
   warms with the glow of radiant light.
   Never again, thinks a changed disciple,
   must we encounter the cold, stark night.

3. Ah! we would stay where the glory thunders,
   worship and pray while the spirit burns,
   if we did not in the mind's eye notice
   how resolutely the Spirit turns.
   Tracing the footsteps that led us upward
   back to the ways where a warmed heart breaks,
   we find compassion and God's hand moving
   on toward the place where a worn world wakes.

From *Songs for the Cycle* © 2004 by Michael Hudson.
Church Publishing Incorporated. All rights reserved. Used by permission.

Meditation for Luke 4.1–13

1 Lent, Year C
The temptation of Christ
87 87
Suggested tune: *Omni die*

1. Now we cease our alleluias
   and more thoughtfully rejoice,
   that with human language muted
   we might hear God's softer voice.

2. Now we leave the shining mountain
   in the company of friends,
   whose encouragement we'll treasure
   as the path we take descends.

3. Now we study Christ's temptations
   in the wilderness alone
   and trust, in the face of evil,
   we'll have answers of our own.

4. Now we set our faces forward,
   following the steps of him
   who with mindfulness and courage
   journeys to Jerusalem.

From *Songs for the Cycle* © 2004 by Michael Hudson.
Church Publishing Incorporated. All rights reserved. Used by permission.

Meditation for Luke 13.31–35

2 Lent, Year C
Jesus continues resolutely toward Jerusalem
11 11 11 5
Suggested tune: *Caelitum Joseph* or *Bickford*

1. A rootless love may flower for a season,
   reaching toward heaven with appealing color;
   and yet before a seed has time to ripen,
   rootless, love withers.

2. A rooted love will grow for many seasons,
   up toward the sunlight, down through Earth's dark goodness,
   out where its branches reach unseeded places;
   rooted, love strengthens.

3. Jesus brings God's love, vital and sustaining,
   into the marrow of a people's spirit,
   out to the structures of a nation's conscience.
   This love is rooted.

From *Songs for the Cycle* © 2004 by Michael Hudson.
Church Publishing Incorporated. All rights reserved. Used by permission.

Meditation for Luke 13.1–9

3 Lent, Year C
Jesus comments on tragedy in the world
10 10 10 10
Suggested tune: *Sursum Corda* or *Morestead*

1. Among the tendrils in the mesh of life
   our stories coil, our spirits rise and twine —
   we are a cell, a seed, a dappled leaf
   in one evolving, interlacing vine.

2. We thought ourselves God's only children once,
   and God a Father with a single care;
   we chafed whenever paths were dark or barbed
   and heaven seemed indifferent or unfair.

3. But we begin to see the way of things —
   a larger family, a cosmosphere
   where God is one who bears creatively
   a grand menagerie of children here.

4. And in this mesh of cause and consequence
   we'll live and hurt and heal and sometimes shine
   and grow with every creature toward this One
   who links and loves us in a common vine.

From *Songs for the Cycle* © 2004 by Michael Hudson.
Church Publishing Incorporated. All rights reserved. Used by permission.

Meditation for Luke 15.11–32

4 Lent, Year C
The prodigal father and son
87 87
Suggested tune: *Charlestown** or *Omni die*

1. Metanoia,** ever-turning,
   re-perceiving where we are,
   glad to orient a footstep
   by a bright and centered star.

2. Metanoia, ever-turning,
   learning always how to learn,
   spreading surfaces toward sunlight
   like a young, uncurling fern.

3. Metanoia, ever-turning,
   graced to make a mindful choice,
   like a child, astray a moment,
   joying in its mother's voice.

4. Metanoia, ever-turning
   to an ever-living Word,
   seeking out the truest telling
   mouth has spoken, ear has heard.

*If *Charlestown* is used, rests should be shortened and notes extended at each line's end.

**Metanoia is the Greek word for repentance.

From *Songs for the Cycle* © 2004 by Michael Hudson.
Church Publishing Incorporated. All rights reserved. Used by permission.

Meditation for Luke 20.9–19

5 Lent, Year C
The unfruitful vineyard
(vis-à-vis evening in the Garden of Eden)
LM
Suggested tune: *Dunedin* or *The River Is Wide*

1. The wind was fresh, the earth was young,
   the scent of life was everywhere,
   the garden lay a fruitful dream
   and God enjoyed the evening air.

2. Where are my loves? the Maker wooed.
   The clay I shape and call by name?
   The question spread through stem and leaf,
   but as God waited, no one came.

3. God's loves were hiding, faces turned,
   beyond the reach of breeze and Voice,
   aware that sometime in the day
   they'd made a dark, far-reaching choice.

4. The question lingers in the leaf,
   in barren branch and shrinking pond—
   Where are my loves? The Maker calls,
   still trusting clay may yet respond.

From *Songs for the Cycle* © 2004 by Michael Hudson.
Church Publishing Incorporated. All rights reserved. Used by permission.

Meditation for Palm Sunday

Year C
Jesus enters Jerusalem
LM
Suggested tune: *Winchester New*

1. We raise our branches high today
   to sign Hosanna and to warn:
   The hands that wield a waving branch
   may also weave a crown of thorns.

2. We sing exultant songs today,
   yet singing we remember this:
   The lips that bring the sweetest praise
   may also bear the sharpest kiss.

3. We greet a golden dawn today
   and marvel as the darkness grows
   that even stalwart confidence
   may fail before the rooster crows.

4. And so our hearts are shaped today
   by palms, a kiss, a friend's denial,
   to hold the very simple prayer —
   God, save us from the time of trial.

From *Songs for the Cycle* © 2004 by Michael Hudson.
Church Publishing Incorporated. All rights reserved. Used by permission.

Meditation for Easter

Year C
77 77
Suggested tune: *Gott sei Dank* or *Bingham*

1. What will rise with Christ today,
   drinking in the April air?
   Scattered forests, gray and bare,
   do these breathe the Easter air?

2. What will rise with Christ today
   gathered into blessèd birth?
   Fur and feather of the earth,
   do these dream of second birth?

3. What will rise with Christ today,
   silencing their enemy?
   Will the creatures of the sea
   leap beside humanity?

4. What will rise with Christ today,
   bringing threatened things in tow?
   Do we, pausing as we grow,
   rise to guide a world in tow?

From *Songs for the Cycle* © 2004 by Michael Hudson.
Church Publishing Incorporated. All rights reserved. Used by permission.

Meditation for John 20.19–31

2 Easter, Years A, B, and C
Jesus appears to Thomas
10 10 10 10
Suggested tune: *Nyack*

1. I have not seen, how am I to believe?
   My eyes have never marked the risen Christ.
   Is one to trust the stories others tell,
   God raising up what has been sacrificed?

2. I have not felt his hands, stone cold, grow warm,
   nor heard the heart once silenced beat again;
   yet here I am, surrounded by a faith
   that apprehends his presence now as then.

3. We hope for signs, but in the end will trust
   that risen Life, arising, surely weaves
   of faith and doubt alike a living truth
   that blesses all who question to believe.

From *Songs for the Cycle* © 2004 by Michael Hudson.
Church Publishing Incorporated. All rights reserved. Used by permission.

Meditation for John 21.1–14

3 Easter, Year C
Jesus reaffirms Peter's vocation
87 87
Suggested tune: *St. Columba*

1. The saints may stumble as they go
   and still the faith advances,
   as in our falling down we find
   a God of second chances.

2. A foot may badly miss a step,
   and still the spirit dances,
   as awkwardness turns to embrace
   a God of second chances.

3. Through fire and failure, faith and doubt,
   in all our circumstances,
   we move with grace because we know
   a God of second chances.

From *Songs for the Cycle* © 2004 by Michael Hudson.
Church Publishing Incorporated. All rights reserved. Used by permission.

Meditation for John 10.22–30

4 Easter, Year C
Hearing the Shepherd's voice
10 10 10 10
Suggested tune: *Sursum Corda*

1. There are no fences in the fields of God,
   an open country greets an endless sky;
   but there are landmarks to direct a step
   and vivid features to engage the eye.

2. We find good pasture on the highest hills
   and streams between alive with water sound
   and groves of trees to shade a sun-scorched back,
   the rich ecology of holy ground.

3. No staff is raised to snatch a wandering sheep;
   we are not branded, hobbled, bound, or belled.
   Yet when we stumble over rock or ledge
   we have a certain sense of being held.

4. There are no fences in the fields of God,
   to come and go is an abiding choice;
   but like the flock before we've come to trust
   the supple tether of a shepherd's voice.

From *Songs for the Cycle* © 2004 by Michael Hudson.
Church Publishing Incorporated. All rights reserved. Used by permission.

Meditation for John 13.31–35

5 Easter, Year C
Love one another that everyone may know...
LM
Suggested tune: *The Eighth Tune*

1. Who has not stood where great waves break
   and felt the deep and ancient ache
   that draws each separate entity
   to step into a boundless sea?

2. Who has not felt the spirit burn
   to love and be loved in return?
   As hollow as a handless glove
   is life that is not touched by love.

3. Who has not stood where lone hearts ache
   and felt compassion surge to break
   whatever boundary sets apart
   the swelling sea and longing heart?

4. Ah, friends of God, we know this Sea!
   The love that fills eternity
   fills us, and who of us cannot
   share, drop by drop, the love of God?

From *Songs for the Cycle* © 2004 by Michael Hudson.
Church Publishing Incorporated. All rights reserved. Used by permission.

Meditation for John 14.23–29

6 Easter, Year C
"Peace I leave with you"
76 76
Suggested tune: *Ave caeli janua*

1. The peace of Christ pervades us,
   between each breath, each thought
   we sense a pulse, a Presence,
   unsummoned and yet sought.

2. The peace of Christ contains us,
   an equipoising force;
   among life's whirring circles
   peace holds us through our course.

3. The peace of Christ extends us
   like tendon coaxing bone
   to reach, a fluid movement,
   toward lives beyond our own.

From *Songs for the Cycle* © 2004 by Michael Hudson.
Church Publishing Incorporated. All rights reserved. Used by permission.

Meditation for John 17.20–26

7 Easter, Year C
(Suitable also for Trinity Sunday)
"...so that they may be one, as we are one,
I in them and you in me..."
10 10 10 10
Suggested tune: *Flentge*

1. The burning love that fired the blood of stars
and arced across creation to combust
as wisdom, peace, and justice through the worlds
still burns and circulates in each of us.

2. The rushing wind that drove the cosmic tide
and swooped to earth to animate our dust
still drives the waves of cosmogenesis
and moves and broods and breathes in each of us.

3. The living water that refreshed the thirst
of simple swimming cells and then was thrust
up through the veins of every living thing
still satisfies the deepest thirst in us.

4. The union of created life and God
eludes our understanding, but we trust
that here and now and through the sweep time
we each exist in God. And God in us.

From *Songs for the Cycle* © 2004 by Michael Hudson.
Church Publishing Incorporated. All rights reserved. Used by permission.

A Meditation Suitable for Trinity Sunday

Long Meter
Suggested tune: *Conditor alme siderum*
or *The Eighth Tune*

1. A narrow door need not exclude
one soul who turns to God today,
but opens to reveal the link
between the near and faraway.

2. As windows in the circled stones
convey a single shaft of light
to strike and mark the crucial point,
a narrow door puts God in sight.

3. And if we have to change our course
or climb or bend and sometimes strain
to catch the light, a child of God
will know it as creative pain.

4. O God, our Source and Goal and Guide,
the Ground we know and yet explore,
you draw us to this opening
and meet us in the narrow door.

From *Songs for the Cycle* © 2004 by Michael Hudson.
Church Publishing Incorporated. All rights reserved. Used by permission.

MEDITATION FOR LUKE 7.1–10

Proper 4, Year C
Jesus heals a Roman officer's servant
CM
Suggested tune: *Irish*

1. A loving heart cannot keep still
   when friends are in great need —
   for love, twined as it is with God,
   exists to intercede.

2. A hopeful heart conspires with God
   and dreams and acts. Or waits.
   And opens to the branching paths
   that hopefulness creates.

3. A vital heart cannot abide
   a dank, unwholesome space —
   We see how Christ infused the world
   with energy and grace.

4. God, give us energy to face
   a needful world wide-eyed
   and step each day into the breach
   where love and need collide.

From *Songs for the Cycle* © 2004 by Michael Hudson.
Church Publishing Incorporated. All rights reserved. Used by permission.

Meditation for Luke 7.11–17

Proper 5, Year C
Jesus raises a woman's son
11 11 11 5
Suggested tune: *Bickford* or *Caelitum Joseph*

1. Where rough injustice chafes a tender people,
   and halls of power offer little wisdom,
   where faith has weakened, finding little nurture,
   hope yet is stirring.

2. Where deep self-interest shapes a common culture,
   and cool disinterest dims a nation's spirit,
   where faith has weakened in compassion's absence,
   love yet is waking.

3. Where wholeness suffers with the strain of living,
   and health drains slowly from the hearts of many,
   faith is rekindled and in Christ's compassion,
   life yet is rising.

From *Songs for the Cycle* © 2004 by Michael Hudson.
Church Publishing Incorporated. All rights reserved. Used by permission.

Meditation for 2 Samuel 11.26ff and Luke 7.36ff

Proper 6, Year C
David and Nathan;
Jesus at the home of Simon the Pharisee
Common Meter Double
Suggested tune: *Kingsfold* or *Halifax*
(See also text for Proper 24, Year A)

1. As David sat, his sins disguised,
   the prophet Nathan came
   to pose the king a parable
   of subtle, double aim.
   The first point drew a royal rage,
   "This man will get his due!"
   The second pierced the royal heart,
   "My king, the man is you."

2. A Pharisee named Simon asked
   a rabbi to a meal,
   to see the storied "Son of Man"
   and pique a "Savior's" zeal.
   Instead he found himself observed
   by wisdom keen enough
   to pose religion's primal choice —
   self-righteousness or love.

3. As David and as Simon did
   as hosts we sit today
   to entertain the word of God
   and all who pass our way.
   And wisdom warns of hosts who love
   the sweetness of control
   and miss the sometimes bitter grace
   by which God feeds the soul.

From *Songs for the Cycle* © 2004 by Michael Hudson.
Church Publishing Incorporated. All rights reserved. Used by permission.

Meditation for Galatians 3.23–29

Proper 7, Year C
Paul teaches, "No Jew or Greek"
Common Meter
Suggested tune: Detroit or Mckee
(For Luke 9.18–24; see also text for Proper 16, Year A, or Proper 19, Year B)

1. Through many ages hands have carved
   in stone their timeless truth;
   in Christ we hear the old stones sing
   that God makes all things new.

2. The Torah, priceless gift of grace,
   set Israel apart,
   yet made it hard to read what God
   was writing on the heart.

3. Paul glimpsed the welling word of God
   and praised it with a vow —
   No Jew or Greek, no slave or free,
   no male or female now!

4. The ancient words leap through the years
   to reach each time and place;
   and Wisdom scans them eagerly
   for God's unfolding grace.

From *Songs for the Cycle* © 2004 by Michael Hudson.
Church Publishing Incorporated. All rights reserved. Used by permission.

Meditation for Luke 9.51–62

Proper 8, Year C
"Come, follow me"
10 10 10 10
Suggested tune: *Sursum Corda*
(See also the text for 2 Epiphany, Year A,
and 4 Lent, Year C)

1. We find in Jesus hope of promised rest —
   "My yoke is gentle and my burden light."
   A darker promise also is expressed,
   and we are wise to keep both thoughts in sight.

2. "Birds have their nests and foxes have their holes,
   the Son of Man no place to lay his head.
   Come, lose a life to find a living soul
   and leave the lifeless to enshrine the dead."

3. Whatever brings us to the God of peace,
   if we remain we meet a God of strife.
   And when both peace and conflict are embraced,
   we come at last to know the God of Life.

From *Songs for the Cycle* © 2004 by Michael Hudson.
Church Publishing Incorporated. All rights reserved. Used by permission.

MEDITATION FOR LUKE 10.1–12

Proper 9, Year C
"The harvest is plentiful but the laborers few"
Common Meter Double
Suggested tune: *Forest Green*

1. A rabbi scattered hope like seeds
   beneath a desert sky;
   he knew in every waking plant
   a sacred force would rise
   to break the ground, to reach for life,
   to search with leaf and root,
   and draw the strength of earth and sky
   to bear the promised fruit.

2. The rabbi saw the desert bloom,
   the Eden of his prayer,
   a garden ripe with hope and life
   and also ripe for care.
   "So come," he says, "my friends, with me
   to tend, to sing, to plod —
   the earth cries out to celebrate
   the greening love of God."

From *Songs for the Cycle* © 2004 by Michael Hudson.
Church Publishing Incorporated. All rights reserved. Used by permission.

Meditation for Luke 10.25–37

Proper 10, Year C
The parable of the Good Samaritan
10 10 10 10
Suggested tune: *Sursum Corda*
(See also the text for Proper 26, Year B)

1. We bring to God the questions of our day,
a steady litany of why and how;
but God is love and as love makes us wise
we often find our questions turned around.

2. "What must I do," a lawyer asked the Lord,
"to enter life?" His question was a test.
"How do you read it?" Jesus gave him time
to see into the truth that he professed.

3. "We must love God with all our heart and soul
and also love our neighbor as we should."
But since he sought to justify himself,
the lawyer sought a smaller neighborhood.

4. "Who is my neighbor then?" the man inquired.
And Jesus told a story in reply
where thoughts of *ally* and *outsider* blurred
and neighborhoods seemed infinitely wide.

5. In open-hearted dialogue with God
there is alarming opportunity
to have our hearts enlarged to see the world
through God's compelling generosity.

From *Songs for the Cycle* © 2004 by Michael Hudson.
Church Publishing Incorporated. All rights reserved. Used by permission.

Meditation for Luke 10.38–42

Proper 11, Year C
Jesus at the home of Mary and Martha
Common Meter Double
Suggested tune: *Resignation*

1. We strive with all our strength and soul
   to do what life requires,
   and somehow while we're on the way
   fulfill our hearts' desires.
   And often as the days speed on
   too hard our small hearts beat.
   Be still, my soul, the Spirit sighs,
   Go sit at Jesus' feet.

2. There is a road we see too well,
   its features fill our eyes;
   a quieter path not far away
   we barely recognize.
   And we must find our way on both,
   or life is incomplete.
   Be still, my soul, the Spirit sighs,
   Go sit at Jesus' feet.

3. The many things we hope to do,
   the wholeness God bestows,
   the center that unites the two
   are closer than one knows.
   There is in us a holy ground
   where prayer and labor meet.
   Be still, my soul, the Spirit sighs,
   Go sit at Jesus' feet.

From *Songs for the Cycle* © 2004 by Michael Hudson.
Church Publishing Incorporated. All rights reserved. Used by permission.

Meditation for Luke 11.1–13

Proper 12, Year C
The Lord's Prayer
87 87 87
Suggested tune: *Julion* or *Lauda anima*

1. God of eager conversation,
   ever wooing us to prayer
   as the primal loving parent
   close beside with constant care,
   though we leap into a mystery,
   still we recognize you there…

2. Energizing life within us,
   feeding us essential bread,
   reconciling life among us,
   tracing mercy's common thread,
   orchestrating life beyond us
   so the Realm of Life is spread.

3. God of lavish affirmation,
   "Seek," you say, and we will find,
   so we seek, and in the seeking
   see the depth of love's design —
   you in us and with us working,
   God and human heart aligned.

From *Songs for the Cycle* © 2004 by Michael Hudson.
Church Publishing Incorporated. All rights reserved. Used by permission.

Meditation for Luke 12.13–21

Proper 13, Year C
The parable of the "Rich Fool"
87 87
Suggested tune: *Omni die*

1. Though the ground groans with its bounty,
   and our arms fill with its fruit,
   it may all add up to nothing
   if we are not rich with you.

2. Though our barns burst with the surplus,
   And we gain more than we use,
   it may all add up to nothing
   if we are not rich with you.

3. Though our hearts swell with assurance,
   and our fate appears approved,
   it may all add up to nothing
   if we are not rich with you.

4. When our lives shine with your blessing,
   and we think, What shall we do?
   Give us grace, God, in the answer,
   that we might be rich with you.

From *Songs for the Cycle* © 2004 by Michael Hudson.
Church Publishing Incorporated. All rights reserved. Used by permission.

Meditation for Luke 12.32–40

Proper 14, Year C
Be ready for the master's return
Long Meter
Suggested tune: The Eighth Tune

1. We watch as all things pass away
   and mark the work of moth and thief;
   our hearts observe and are concerned
   that life is brittle and is brief.

2. And so we work to build a life
   that stands the famine and the flood;
   we sow and gather, seize and hoard —
   it is the instinct of our blood.

3. But there is other instinct here,
   a wisdom drawing hearts to truth —
   life grows less bounded and more full
   when we are watching, God, for you.

4. So come, our Wisdom, when you will
   and urge us each in time and space
   beyond our primal, grasping need
   and on toward your unfolding grace.

From *Songs for the Cycle* © 2004 by Michael Hudson.
Church Publishing Incorporated. All rights reserved. Used by permission.

Meditation for Luke 12.49–56

Proper 15, Year C
"I have not come to bring peace"
Common Meter
Suggested tune: *St. Anne*
(See also the texts for 2 Advent
and 3 Epiphany, Year C)

1. When Jesus tells his friends he comes
   to set the earth ablaze,
   it must at least be wise to pause
   and ask what he would raze.

2. When Jesus tells his friends he comes
   to sever and estrange,
   it must at least be wise to learn
   what he intends to change.

3. When Jesus tells his friends he comes
   that crisis might increase,
   it must, it must be time to seek
   a wider, deeper peace.

From *Songs for the Cycle* © 2004 by Michael Hudson.
Church Publishing Incorporated. All rights reserved. Used by permission.

MEDITATION FOR LUKE 13.22–30

Proper 16, Year C
"Strive to enter through the narrow door..."
Long Meter
Suggested tune: *Conditor alme siderum*
or *The Eighth Tune*

1. A narrow door need not exclude
   one soul who turns to God today,
   but opens to reveal the link
   between the near and faraway.

2. As windows in the circled stones
   convey a single shaft of light
   to strike and mark the crucial point,
   a narrow door puts God in sight.

3. And if we have to change our course
   or climb or bend and sometimes strain
   to catch the light, a child of God
   will know it as creative pain.

4. O God, our Source and Goal and Guide,
   the Ground we know and yet explore,
   you draw us to this opening
   and meet us in the narrow door.

From *Songs for the Cycle* © 2004 by Michael Hudson.
Church Publishing Incorporated. All rights reserved. Used by permission.

Meditation for Luke 14.1,7–14

Proper 17, Year C
Wisdom for guests and hosts
Common Meter Double
Suggested tune: *Halifax*
(See also the text for Proper 23, Year A)

1 If life is like a wedding feast
   and we are cast as guests,
   then it is tragic not to know
   the life God manifests.
   Distracted by appearances,
   seduced by praise or place,
   if we remain outside ourselves
   we miss this moment's grace.

2 If life is like a wedding feast
   and we are cast as hosts,
   then it is limiting to list
   the ones we like the most
   and leave apart, outside, unknown
   uncounted other souls,
   when love suggests there is no feast
   till all the parts are whole.

3 And God is making life a feast,
   embracing us as guests
   so that with self-forgetting grace
   we gather and are blessed
   to taste and know that God is good
   and spreads the table wide,
   so wide we know to say with God,
   Come, all my friends, inside.

From *Songs for the Cycle* © 2004 by Michael Hudson.
Church Publishing Incorporated. All rights reserved. Used by permission.

Meditation for Luke 14.25–33

Proper 18, Year C
Balance in relationships, self, and things
98 98 D
Suggested tune: *Rendez à Dieu*
(See also the text for Proper 11, Year B)

1. Tracing the swirling stars above us,
   sensing the molten core below,
   feet in the dust and hands uplifted,
   most gracious God, in you we know
   that at the point between the powers
   which form and flash and pulse and pound,
   consciousness grows to meet its Maker,
   here in the blessed middle ground.

2. Reaching to taste the fruit of knowledge,
   marked by the gift forevermore,
   we feel the separating distance
   between each near and farther shore;
   and so we flee the love of others
   or wind our cords too tightly round
   without your reconciling Presence,
   here in the blessed middle ground.

3. Even within ourselves we waver
   between the tides of mind and soul;
   and in the world of things we wither,
   consumption fed beyond control.
   Creating God and holy Center
   within all powers that confound—
   be with us as a living balance,
   here in the blessed middle ground.

From *Songs for the Cycle* © 2004 by Michael Hudson.
Church Publishing Incorporated. All rights reserved. Used by permission.

Meditation for Luke 15.1–10

Proper 19, Year C
Jesus seeks the lost
Long Meter
Suggested tune: *Winchester New*

1. Converging as potential friends,
   the sinful and their God drew near
   and would at once have made a feast
   had not the righteous interfered.

2. The rabbi Jesus linked the two —
   a loving God with eager hearts.
   Religion in its darker form
   contrived to keep the two apart.

3. But love from God is strong and wide,
   it seeks and finds and celebrates
   the good, the bad, the in-between
   who turn and take what love creates.

4. Now we have heard the song of God
   rejoicing over us as friends;
   and we, as bent but mending saints,
   must choose how far this love extends.

From *Songs for the Cycle* © 2004 by Michael Hudson.
Church Publishing Incorporated. All rights reserved. Used by permission.

MEDITATION FOR LUKE 16.1–13

Proper 20, Year C
The parable of the shrewd manager
Common Meter
Suggested tune: *Mckee*

1. How would we use the wealth of God
   if it were ours today,
   what wisdom would we find that tells
   how much to give away?

2. Is there a limit to the Source,
   a reason not to spend
   the currency of love and life
   in making strangers friends?

3. We know that God is prodigal
   with justice, peace, and love;
   the trouble comes enlisting help
   to spend them fast enough.

4. Can we, in partnership with God,
   be trusted then to waste,
   to lavish, spread, fling far too wide
   the riches of God's grace?

From *Songs for the Cycle* © 2004 by Michael Hudson.
Church Publishing Incorporated. All rights reserved. Used by permission.

Meditation for Luke 16.19–31

Proper 21, Year C
The rich man and Lazarus
98 98 Double
Suggested tune: *Rendez à Dieu*

1 Come! Sing the bells of invitation,
   come while the summons resonates;
   enter, enjoy the fruit of Spirit
   spread so that all participate.
   Here, as the saints prepare to enter,
   each heart attuned to celebrate,
   eyes raised to God, may we yet notice
   the stranger waiting at the gate.

2 Wisdom has taught us, Count your blessings.
   We count, God sets a gracious plate.
   And with it sets an open table;
   this, too, the wise appreciate.
   God, give us windows with your mercies,
   that mercy never insulates
   and hides our partner in the blessing,
   the stranger waiting at the gate.

3 Hear! Sing the bells of indignation,
   hear through the stories love narrates.
   God sees a day for trading places
   between the humble and the great.
   Great is the hope God breathes upon us
   that, rooted, grace will radiate
   as saints make places at the table
   for strangers waiting at the gate.

From *Songs for the Cycle* © 2004 by Michael Hudson.
Church Publishing Incorporated. All rights reserved. Used by permission.

Meditation for Luke 17.5–10

Proper 22, Year C
"Lord, increase our faith"
76 76 76
Suggested tune: *Dix*

1. Jesus saw a different world
than the settled world we know;
he said faith can plant a tree
in the waves and it will grow.
Give us, God, a heart to see
both what is and what can be.

2. Jesus saw a different world
than the settled world we know;
he said in the driest lives
deep, refreshing streams would flow.
Give us, God, a heart to see
both what is and what can be.

3. Jesus saw a different world
than the settled world we know,
pulsing with a latent grace,
face of God in embryo.
Give us, God, a heart to see
both what is and what can be.

From *Songs for the Cycle* © 2004 by Michael Hudson.
Church Publishing Incorporated. All rights reserved. Used by permission.

Meditation for Luke 17.11–19

Proper 23, Year C
Ten lepers are healed
LM
Suggested tune: *The Eighth Tune*

1 Our wounds may best prepare our hearts
  to see beyond the known and near —
  ten lepers watched the Lord approach
  and spoke their hopes for all to hear.

2 As always Jesus' heart was stirred,
  requiting eagerness with grace;
  he sent the ten to give the priests
  a glimpse of new creation's face.

3 And as they went the healing took —
  their skin, their health, their lives restored.
  Nine men went on to find the priests,
  the tenth went back to bless the Lord.

4 And he the only foreigner,
  the one least known, least loved, most odd;
  yet he, perhaps, the best prepared
  to recognize the face of God.

From *Songs for the Cycle* © 2004 by Michael Hudson.
Church Publishing Incorporated. All rights reserved. Used by permission.

Meditation for Luke 18.1–8a

Proper 24, Year C
The persistent widow
98 98 88
Suggested tune: *Wer nur den lieben Gott*
(also known as *Neumark*)

1. Jesus describes a forceful woman,
   a widow who refused to bend
   before a judge, a man of power,
   whose judgments worked to no good end.
   She knew that she had power, too,
   and trusted in the strength she knew.

2. And day by day she spoke for justice,
   and word by word injustice waned
   until impassive will relented
   and her impassioned faith remained.
   Believing God would make a way,
   she found the grace that faith conveys.

3. Now we, observing, are invited
   to recollect what faith can gain
   when faithful people are undaunted
   and hope, in conflict, is sustained.
   As we, like she, wield stubborn trust,
   God comes to move the world through us.

From *Songs for the Cycle* © 2004 by Michael Hudson.
Church Publishing Incorporated. All rights reserved. Used by permission.

Meditation for Luke 18.9–14

Proper 25, Year C
The Pharisee and toll-collector
77 77 77
Suggested tune: *Ratisbon*

1. Two men came to God in prayer,
   one was thankful, one was pained.
   One man pious, practiced, pure;
   one uncertain, shaken, stained.
   Each told something of his heart
   as he stood or stood apart.

2. Drawing near the first man prayed—
   "Thank you, Lord, I'm not like him."
   Hesitant, the other's cry
   rang out as an antonym—
   "God, have mercy if you can
   on a straying, broken man."

3. Sometimes we must think God takes
   more delight in polished souls,
   as we smooth ourselves to seem
   good, enlightened, faithful, whole.
   Jesus cleared this stifling air,
   saying, "Trust the sinner's prayer."

4. Loving God, when we yet choose
   piety that makes us numb,
   owning that we surely need
   grace, but not as much as some,
   help us know a sinner's trust
   profits even saints like us.

From *Songs for the Cycle* © 2004 by Michael Hudson.
Church Publishing Incorporated. All rights reserved. Used by permission.

Meditation for Luke 19.1–10

Proper 26, Year C
Jesus and Zacchaeus
Long Meter
Suggested tune: *The Eighth Tune*

1. A man not known for sacred sense
sensed something sacred close at hand,
and hedged by taller heads around,
was desperate for a place to stand.

2. Zacchaeus climbed the nearest tree,
expectant, as his instinct urged
and watched and waited there as hope
and opportunity converged.

3. One face looked up and one looked down,
and each saw in the other's eye
both window for the grace of God
and reason not to pass it by.

4. The angels may have sung that day,
the trees may well have clapped their hands —
creation cheers the eagerness
that seeks a surer place to stand.

From *Songs for the Cycle* © 2004 by Michael Hudson.
Church Publishing Incorporated. All rights reserved. Used by permission.

Meditation for Luke 20.27–38

Proper 27, Year C
The Sadducees question Jesus about Resurrection
Common Meter Double
Suggested tune: *Kingsfold*

1. As Moses flees a nation's shame
   he comes or else is sent
   to gaze into the fire of God
   that burns but is not spent.
   And here his own soul's way is forged,
   from this day he will sense
   the fire, the grace, the Name of God
   in ever-present tense.

2. As Job sits broken in the dust
   to voice his heart's complaint,
   he shakes an honest, probing fist
   for every broken saint.
   His questions are unanswered, yet
   his quest is purposive—
   he sits, unknowing, till he knows
   that his Redeemer lives.

3. As Jesus gains Jerusalem
   where prophet's blood is shed,
   he speaks of everlasting life
   with those who wish him dead.
   He knows the law, the truth, the risk
   to tread where prophets trod,
   and knows the ever-present hope
   of hearts alive to God.

From *Songs for the Cycle* © 2004 by Michael Hudson.
Church Publishing Incorporated. All rights reserved. Used by permission.

MEDITATION FOR LUKE 21.5–19

Proper 28, Year C
Seasons and signs
77 77 77
Suggested tune: *Ratisbon*
(See also the text for 1 Advent, Year C)

1. At the turning of the year
   we return to contemplate
   seasons, cycles, signs, and times,
   sacred ground to cultivate.
   Insight often grows more clear
   at the turning of the year.

2. At the turning of the year
   waxing nights annunciate
   warmer suns that promise spring,
   even as the sun migrates.
   Hope sleeps in the husk of fear
   at the turning of the year.

3. At the turning of the year
   we look back and speculate
   on the ebb and flow of life,
   asking what it indicates.
   Wisdom speaks, and some will hear
   at the turning of the year.

4. At the turning of the year
   we look forward as we wait
   for the grace of God in time,
   never early, never late,
   always distant, always here
   at the turning of the year.

From *Songs for the Cycle* © 2004 by Michael Hudson.
Church Publishing Incorporated. All rights reserved. Used by permission.

Meditation for Luke 19.29–38

Proper 29, Year C
Jesus enters Jerusalem
Common Meter Double
Suggested tune: *Ton-y-Botel*
(See also the text for Proper 29, Year A)

1. Down the ages saints ascended
to Jerusalem to bring
songs and psalms of expectation
for the long-expected king.
Cry hosanna, high hosannas!
Join the pilgrims as they sing.
Lift your voices, cry hosanna
for the long-expected king!

2. Christ comes riding on a donkey
toward the buoyant clamoring;
cloaks and praise are spread as honor
for the long-expected king.
Cry hosanna, high hosannas,
hard the heart that does not sing.
Lift your voices, cry hosanna
for the long-expected king!

3. Prophecies, in faith remembered,
into flesh and spirit spring;
all the gathered weight of glory
greets the long-expected king.
Cry hosanna, high hosannas,
stones themselves are poised to sing.
Lift your voices, cry hosanna
for the long-expected king!

4. Songs of saints will rise and waver,
incomplete our offering;
then and now the praise inconstant
for the long-expected king.
Cry hosanna, high hosannas,
our unfinished songs yet ring.
Lift your voices, cry hosanna
for the long-expected king!

From *Songs for the Cycle* © 2004 by Michael Hudson.
Church Publishing Incorporated. All rights reserved. Used by permission.

ADDITIONAL HYMNS FOR THE REVISED COMMON LECTIONARY

MEDITATION FOR LUKE 7.36–50

Proper 6(11) Year C (RCL)
A woman anoints Jesus' feet
with ointment and tears
11 10 11 10
Suggested tune: *Charterhouse*

1. Sometimes with God we sense a silent presence,
   the wordless music of a windless night,
   pervasive as the force that binds our atoms
   and unobtrusive as the moon's gray light.

2. Sometimes we have a flooding of emotion,
   a gratitude so potent that we weep
   and watch our tears fall on the feet of Jesus,
   amazed, as deep is calling out to deep.

3. Sometimes we sense God's presence in an action,
   a kindness done, injustice met with deeds
   charged with the strength and beauty of compassion—
   faith taking flesh to follow where Christ leads.

4. In all our times, whether or not we know it,
   God holds us in a womb, a thought, a hand,
   a universe alive with grace and purpose,
   as consciousness evolves to understand.

From *Songs for the Cycle* © 2004 by Michael Hudson.
Church Publishing Incorporated. All rights reserved. Used by permission.

Meditation for Matthew 28.1–10

Easter Vigil, Year A (RCL)
The angels tell the disciples
that Christ awaits them in Galilee
77 77
Suggested tune: Gott sei dank

1 Life moves forward. So must we
rise and go as morning spreads.
Though our backs are bent with grief,
Christ awaits us on ahead.

2 Life moves forward. So must we
find our path and move, God-sped.
Though our energy is spent,
Christ awaits us on ahead.

3 Life moves forward. So must we
trust in what the angels said.
Though we last were with him here,
Christ awaits us on ahead.

4 Life moves forward. So must we
leave the dead to mourn the dead.
Love is risen. We are called.
Christ awaits us on ahead.

From *Songs for the Cycle* © 2004 by Michael Hudson.
Church Publishing Incorporated. All rights reserved. Used by permission.

Index of Hymn Tunes

Adoro devote, 22, 55, 91
Aus der Tiefe rufe ich, 113, 122
Ave caeli janua, 12, 56, 72, 147
Bickford, 114, 133, 137, 151
Bingham, 64, 78, 112, 142
Brother James' Air, 80
Caelites plaudant, 102
Caelitum Joseph, 137, 151
Charlestown, 65, 139
Charterhouse, 130, 176
Come Holy Ghost, 33
Conditor alme siderum, 92, 95, 149, 162
Coventry Carol, 82
Cradle Song, 99
Danby, 101
Deirdre, 109
Detroit, 88, 153
Deus tuorum militum, 58
Dickinson College, 35, 50, 117
Divinum mysterium, 89
Dix, 10, 168
Dundee, 18, 31, 93, 106, 131
Dunedin, 140
Engelberg, 128
Faith, 132
Flentge, 44, 48, 59, 68, 70, 118, 148
Forest Green, 13, 155
Foundation, 29
Franconia, 123
Georgetown, 28
Gott sei Dank, 78, 113, 142, 177
Halifax, 8, 13, 125, 152, 163
Halton Holgate, 98
Holy Manna, 96
Irby, 87
Irish, 39, 94, 150
Julion, 16, 158
Kingsfold, 8, 27, 51, 79, 125, 152, 173
Land of Rest, 54
Lauda anima, 16, 158
Laudate Dominum, 97
Love Unknown, 84
Lytlington, 129

Mckee, 153, 166
Morestead, 138
Morning Tune, 80
Nettleton, 19, 66, 134
Neumark. *See* Wer nur den lieben Gott
Noël nouvelet, 100
Nun komm, der Heiden Heiland, 64, 107
Nyack, 23, 43, 59, 85, 143
Omni die, 14, 30, 45, 74, 77, 81, 116, 121, 127, 136, 139, 159
Pleading Savior, 15, 135
Puer nobis, 37, 73
Quam dilecta, 63, 105
Ratisbon, 3, 20, 171, 174
Rendez à Dieu, 164, 167
Resignation, 157
Restoration, 26, 90, 127
St. Anne, 5, 6, 28, 36, 42, 47, 53, 161
St. Cecilia, 63, 69
St. Columba, 40, 144
St. Denio, 29, 76
St. Flavian, 17, 53, 131
St. Flavian (original rhythm), 5
St. Stephen, 6
Salvation, 79
Shalom chevarim, 32
Slane, 103, 111
Star of the County Down, 51
Stuttgart, 14, 26, 45, 65, 74, 121
Sursum Corda, 4, 38, 44, 46, 68, 70, 71, 104, 108, 138, 145, 154, 156
Tallis' Ordinal, 7
Tender Thought, 115
The Call, 67, 110
The Eighth Tune, 9, 24, 25, 41, 49, 52, 57, 73, 92, 124, 126, 146, 149, 160, 162, 169, 172
The Water Is Wide, 11
Ton-y-Botel, 175
Wem in Leidenstagen, 75, 86
Wer nur den lieben Gott, 170
Winchester New, 9, 21, 34, 50, 58, 83, 124, 126, 141, 165

Thematic Index

Baptism
2 Lent, Year A: A font evokes the womb of God, 17
1 Epiphany, Year B: Let rain come down today, 69
1 Epiphany, Year C: Something stirs when heaven opens, 127
5 Easter, Year C: Who has not stood where great waves break, 146

Children (texts appropriate for)
Proper 24, Year A, option #2: What shall we give to God who gives, 54
4 Easter, Year B: David was a daring shepherd, 87

Creation
Proper 11, Year A: The roots of all things interweave, 40
6 Easter, Year B: From a time beyond beginnings, 89
Proper 6, Year B: There is a goodness in the ground, 95
Proper 8, Year B: God's love, like a stream, 97
Proper 21, Year B: Bless the good wherever it grows, 110
Proper 23, Year B: Brother Sun and Sister Moon, 112
3 Lent, Year C: Among the tendrils in the mesh of life, 138
4 Lent, Year C: Metanoia, ever-turning, 139
5 Lent, Year C: The wind was fresh, the earth was young, 140
Easter, Year C: What will rise with Christ today, 142
7 Easter, Year C: The burning love that fired the blood of stars, 148
Proper 9, Year C: A rabbi scattered hope like seeds, 155

The Cross
Proper 17, Year A: The way to Life takes unexpected turns, 46
5 Lent, Year B: Fall to the earth, small solitary seed, 82

Eucharist
Proper 13, Year A: When circumstances drain the soul, 42
Proper 23, Year A: Before the morning light has passed, 52
8 Epiphany, Year B: Today we are gathered to join in a feast, 76
4 Lent, Year B: Jesus watched us from a mountain, 81
Proper 11, Year B: Taking what is given, 100
Proper 13, Year B: New every morning is our human yearning, 102
Proper 15, Year B: The gifts we have presented move toward God, 104

Faith and Trust
Proper 14, Year A: There will be times when Christ seems far away, 43
Proper 15, Year A: A Gentile woman came to Christ to glean, 44

Proper 22, Year C: Jesus saw a different world, 168
Proper 25, Year C: Two men came to God in prayer, 171

Forgiveness

Proper 19, Year A: Forgiveness is a given with the Lord, 48
3 Easter, Year C: The saints may stumble as they go, 144

The Holy Spirit

Pentecost, Year A: Fresh fire falls from heaven, 29
1 Advent, Year B: A patient presence broods, 63
4 Advent, Year B: Countless prayers of faithful people, 66
8 Epiphany, Year B: Today we are gathered to join in a feast, 76
3 Easter, Year B: Present, though unlooked for, 86
5 Easter, Year B: There is a song the Spirit sings, 88
Proper 9, Year B: Hidden in the ordinary, 98
1 Epiphany, Year C: Something stirs when heaven opens, 127
3 Epiphany, Year C: Christ, be now the voice that heartens the impoverished, 129

Justice

Proper 5, Year A: Why is it that the friends of God, 34
Proper 20, Year A: A bright, unsympathetic sun, 49
3 Epiphany, Year C: Christ, be now the voice that heartens the impoverished, 129
6 Epiphany, Year C: Blessed are we poor, for it is God's desire, 132
Proper 5, Year C: Where rough injustice chafes a tender people, 151
Proper 24, Year C: Jesus describes a forceful woman, 170

Marriage

Proper 22, Year B: Love is a longing, a flame in the night, 111

Mission

Last Epiphany, Year A: Sometimes we come to the soul's high places, 15
Proper 16, Year A: What do people say of Jesus, 45
7 Easter, Year B: In the comfort that we cling to, 90
Proper 7, Year B: There's a land across the water, 96
Proper 10, Year B: A road at our doorstep, 99
Proper 18, Year B: Fishers fishing not for fish, 107
Proper 21, Year B: Bless the good wherever it grows, 110
Proper 24, Year B: Wisdom makes a way to God, 113
3 Epiphany, Year C: Christ, be now the voice that heartens the impoverished, 129
4 Epiphany, Year C: Rain often falls across the distant mountains, 130
5 Easter, Year C: Who has not stood where great waves break, 146
6 Easter, Year C: The peace of Christ pervades us, 147
Proper 4, Year C: A loving heart cannot keep still, 150
Proper 9, Year C: A rabbi scattered hope like seeds, 155

Thematic Index

Proper 16, Year C: A narrow door need not exclude, 162
Proper 19, Year C: Converging as potential friends, 165

Mystery

Pentecost, Year B: To the edge of oceans where waves engage stone, 91
Proper 12, Year B: Into the night Christ sent his friends, 101
Proper 17, Year B: The Church's lasting paradox, 106
Proper 20, Year B: In the tangle of our living, 109
4 Epiphany, Year C: Rain often falls across the distant mountains, 130
Proper 23, Year C: Our wounds may best prepare our hearts, 169

Prayer and Meditation

2 Advent, Year A: Our road runs through a wilderness, 5
4 Easter, Year A: Among the day's competing sounds, 25
Proper 6, Year A: Our better prayers begin as love, 35
6 Epiphany, Year B: Silence is a way of holding, 74
Proper 16, Year B: You have the words of life, 105
Proper 26, Year B: God, I would love you with all my heart, 115
Proper 28, Year B: When apprehension frets the soul, 117
5 Epiphany, Year C: A prayer can ride a breath, exhaled, 131
Last Epiphany, Year A: Sometimes we come to the soul's high places, 15
5 Easter, Year C: Who has not stood where great waves break, 146
Proper 4, Year C: A loving heart cannot keep still, 150
Proper 11, Year C: We strive with all our strength and soul, 157
Proper 12, Year C: God of eager conversation, 158
Proper 24, Year C: Jesus describes a forceful woman, 170

The Realm of God

Proper 22, Year A: Because we do not see the One, 51
Proper 27, Year A: A long obedience is asked, 57
Proper 29, Year A: O Jesus, we have tried to make you king, 59
1 Advent, Year B: A patient presence broods, 63
6 Easter, Year B: From a time beyond beginnings, 89
1 Advent, Year C: Though the fig tree does not blossom, 121
4 Easter, Year C: There are no fences in the fields of God, 145
Proper 14, Year C: We watch as all things pass away, 160

Repentance

Proper 26, Year A: There is a hope of turning, 56
4 Lent, Year C: Metanoia, ever-turning, 139
5 Lent, Year C: The wind was fresh, the earth was young, 140

Servant Leadership

Proper 24, Year B: Wisdom makes a way to God, 113

Stewardship

Proper 28, Year A: To think like Jesus is to risk, 58
Proper 11, Year B: Taking what is given, 100
Proper 27, Year B: Simple gifts of faithful people, 116
5 Epiphany, Year C: A prayer can ride a breath, exhaled, 131
Proper 13, Year C: Though the ground groans with its bounty, 159
Proper 20, Year C: How would we use the wealth of God, 166

Wisdom

Proper 24, Year A, option #1: The foolish set a snare for God, 53
Proper 25, Year A: Many choices meet us, moving through the day, 55
3 Advent, Year B: In the winters early darkness, 65
7 Epiphany, Year B: Life presents the puzzles, 75
Proper 24, Year B: Wisdom makes a way to God, 113
2 Epiphany, Year C: When simple mirth and joyfulness decline, 128
7 Epiphany, Year C: Time rounds with choices, 133